CLASSICAL ARCHITECTURE
The Poetics of Order

Alexander Tzonis and Liane Lefaivre

The MIT Press
Cambridge, Massachusetts
London, England

This publication draws in part from *De Taal van de Klassicistiese Architektuur* (Nijmegen: SUN, 1984). © Alexander Tzonis and Liane Lefaivre. This edition included as co-author Denis Bilodeau. Leo de Bruin was the graphic designer.

Eighth printing, 1997

This book was set in Sabon by Achorn Graphics and printed and bound in the United States of America.

Library of Congress Cataloging-in-Publication Data

Tzonis, Alexander.
    Classical architecture.

    "This publication draws in part from De taal van de klassicistiese architektuur"—T.p. verso.
    Bibliography: p.
    Includes index.
    1. Architecture, Classical. 2. Architecture—Orders. I. Lefaivre, Liane. II. Tzonis, Alexander. De taal van de klassicistiese architektuur. III. Title.
NA260.T96   1986   722'.8   86-5397
ISBN 0-262-70031-X

To the memory of Hariclea Xanthopoulou-Tzoni (1906–1983)

CONTENTS

Preface and Acknowledgments

This book investigates the poetics of classical architecture. It studies the canon, that is, how classical buildings are put together as formal structures, and it studies how such structures produce a tragic discourse and become pieces of public art with critical, moral, and philosophical meaning. We believe that this approach complements those that have focused on classical buildings as symbolic or tectonic objects. Our work has resulted from an effort to understand the secret of classical architecture's eternal youth, a quality it shares with classical music, literature, and painting. But it is also the outcome of a critical response to some current uses of classical architecture. We believe that, if returning to classical architecture is to make any sense today, it must be as a way of reflecting on the classical humanist tradition from which it springs.

The material in this book was drawn from a number of libraries whose help we would like to acknowledge: the Library of the Architecture Department of the Technische Hogeschool Delft, the Blackader Library of McGill University, the Loeb Library at the Harvard Graduate School of Design, and the Library of the Kunsthistorisch Instituut of the University of Utrecht.

The book originates in part from *De Taal van de Klassicistiese Architektuur* (Nijmegen: SUN, 1983), a much shorter publication. Special thanks should be given to Denis Bilodeau for his assistance in the domain of visual documentation to that earlier publication; to the Dutch-Canadian bilateral cultural exchange program, which made possible his presence in the Department of Architecture of the Technische Hogeschool Delft; and to the department itself, which covered the cost of the visual documentation. The research was also partially carried out in the framework of the Voorwaardelijke Financiering Program of the Dutch government. In addition, we would like to thank Maike van Dieten, Leo de Bruin, Tjef van der Wiel, and in particular Henk Hoeks of our Dutch publisher SUN for their enthusiastic support and their excellent technical contribution to this initial undertaking. We are grateful to James Ackerman, Kenneth Frampton, Phyllis Lambert, Pierre-André Michel, Robert Oxman, Ed Taverne for patient and incisive comments, and to Robert Berwick, who shaped the book in ways he might not even be aware of. Eric Offermans contributed in updating the visual material. Sonja Spiekerman and Paola van Hijkoop typed the manuscript with patience and rigor. Finally, we wish to express our special appreciation to our editor, Roger Conover, for his tireless care and encouragement.

CLASSICAL ARCHITECTURE

Diotima lives on, like tender blooms in mid-winter,
Full of essential spirit, and seeking out the sun,
Although the sun of the spirit, the more beautiful world, has sunk.
And in the frozen night, blizzards only lash out at one another.

Friedrich Hölderlin, *Diotima* (1798)

It is the Acropolis that made a rebel of me. One clear image will stand in my
mind forever: the Parthenon. Stark, stripped, economical, violent; a clamorous
outcry against a landscape of grace and terror. All strength and purity.

Le Corbusier, Fourth Meeting of the CIAM, 1933

Logos Opticos: The Logic of Composition

Classical architecture, like any other product of culture, is a social phenomenon. The origin of the term is telling. *Classical* means related to the social order of the *classici,* the highest rank of the hierarchical social structure of ancient Rome, juxtaposed to the lowest, that of the *proletarii.* One could demonstrate in many other ways the relation between classical architecture and society, starting with classical architecture's obsession with rigorous quantification, exactitude, and detail. This obsession has its roots in what anthropologists and historians call divinatory thinking, typical of tribal societies. The *temenos,* the meticulously ordered temple precinct dedicated to a god or hero in archaic Greece, is the product of such divinatory thinking, governed as it is by taboos of pollution and the cult of purity. One could show how the divinatory role of archaic temples gradually declined, giving way to a different, new, modern, aesthetic role with the rise of the Athenian empire. Inversely, one could also indicate how archaic concepts of architectural composition resurfaced during the Middle Ages and early Renaissance. One could associate these changes in architectural thinking with the vicissitudes of the money economy in Europe, the emergence of new social formations and new institutions, the birth of court culture and the reopening of world market routes, the invention of credit institutions, and the need to educate a nascent elite in such new ideas as the worth of time and profit. Finally, one could establish how classical architecture served to bolster new forms of power, first republican, then absolutist.

Thanks to the considerable efforts of researchers during the past few decades, especially since the Second World War, we have some good knowledge about how classical architecture was linked with such social and political developments. But when it comes to looking at classical architecture from the point of view of poetics, from the point of view of composition—the term *poetics* derives from the ancient Greek verb to make, *poiéin,* and applies not only to poetry but to every kind of intellectual and manual production—we still rely heavily on the results of the pioneering work of few scholars in *Kunstwissenschaft,* such as Wölfflin (1888, 1899) and Frankl (1936, 1968). Little work has been carried out in the last half century on how one composes a classical building or what inferences one makes when one looks at such a building and says this is well formed, this is classical.

This book inquires into just how classical architecture is made, how it works as a *formal system.* It analyzes buildings as *compositions* from a *visual, morphological,* or *stylistic* point of view. It tries to identify the kind of logic associated with this system, what Vitruvius called the *logos opticos* (*De Architectura,* bk. I, ch. I, para. 16). Once this study is carried out, the essay turns to the investigation of the general basic mechanisms through which formal composition carries meaning and acquires a social use, what we refer to as the critical use of classical architecture.

Purely formal studies such as the one we undertake in the first part of this essay, of course, always invite basic questions. Is the formal organization of buildings a goal in itself or is it a vehicle for a particular meaning or social purpose, a subordinate of a larger task. Can buildings be studied as formal objects only? To this we must answer immediately that focusing on the formal aspects of classical architecture has its own limitations and dangers as a methodological undertaking. It is easy for a formal analysis to slip into formalism; to adopt the idea that purely optical norms are the only determinants of architecture and that there is a will to form above and beyond social life and material constraints. It is easy for formal analysis to envision what Focillon called the "world of forms" as a "place to dream superior and free" (1948); and to take for granted that what Kubler (1962) identified as "the system for formal relations" and what Panofsky (1939) called "the world of artistic motifs" are not methodological hypotheses but autonomous realities. These are indeed reductive hypotheses. They result in limiting our understanding of classical architecture by assigning to form in architecture a larger role than it actually plays.

To avoid such fallacies, one should keep in mind that formal analysis alone can be only descriptive. It may lead to some general conclusions about phenomena of form, but it cannot explain, let alone give direction to, the actual practice of architecture. Left to itself, it cannot relate formal norms to the cognitive social norms that ultimately give meaning and purpose to architecture.

The isolation of formal aspects and their independent analysis is necessary, however, if one is interested in understanding classical architecture as a coherent system rather than as a haphazard collection of shapes and details. It offers a deep comprehension of how a building is made, which is different from how it is used, and what impact it has.

Once we accept the need for formal analysis, the question arises, From where will the categories of such an analysis derive? It is evident that any formal stylistic inquiry into classical architecture runs the risk of being a mere reflection of our contemporary reactions and thus of producing trivial results. This is the case when we rely on "psychological" concepts that are supposed to express emotions ("surprise," "variety," "excitement," "awe," "clarity") or "qualities" of space ("large or small scale," "thrusting masses," "heavy volumes," "floating spaces," "mysterious vistas," "transparencies," "twilight depths"). Useful as such expressions might be in communicating metaphorically what a viewer might feel about an architectural work, they yield next to nothing about the nature of classical architecture as a formal system.

These concepts refer to the psychological, emotional states that result from the forms, but they hardly describe the forms themselves. It is easy to demonstrate not only historically but also experimentally how different forms elicit the same psychological effect and, conversely, how the same forms tend to elicit different psychological effects. Such concepts not only are ambiguous but also make no claim to represent authentically the knowledge that exists in the minds of the designers or the viewers of classical buildings, making the creation and appreciation of these buildings possible.

The first step toward representing this knowledge is to go back to the documents of the periods in which classical architecture was shaped in order to find out how classical architecture was seen, how it was talked about, and what the categories are through which classical buildings were originally conceived and perceived. In this way we can identify the formal system in the making or still under discussion. Once a system was adopted, its rules gradually became unconscious, even among the architecturally literate public, and their norms completely internalized, thus invisible.

Although our task is to construct an operational definition of classical architecture and not to reconstruct a historical epistemology of its conceptual framework, there is a pressing need to go back to the documentary sources of the generic periods of classical architecture. These sources are writings that have clearly displayed the categories of formal analysis, such as Vitruvius's *De Architectura,* a straightforward text on architecture, unique for its systematic approach and its encyclopedic outlook. We know that it was the practice for architects to write a commentary about each of their buildings. Vitruvius cites seventeen of them, including that of the great Iktinos on the Parthenon, Pythius on the Temple of Athena Polias in Priene and the Mausoleum of Hallicarnassos, and Hermogenes on the Temple of Diana in Magnesia (*De Architectura,* bk. VII, Introduction). We have to rely on Vitruvius because, alas, none of these texts on architecture have survived.

Classical texts on poetics and rhetoric, which can be applied to architecture indirectly, are also important. Our reckoning of such texts follows from the central role that such material played in forming the mind of the educated public or in reflecting what was in the mind of such people, in antiquity and since the Renaissance up to the end of the ancien régime. Poetics and rhetoric were the backbone of the humanist culture that gave birth to classical music and classical literature as well as to classical architecture. Within the humanist circles the study of Aristotle, Cicero, and Quintilian was everyday fare.

Aristotle and the other theoreticians of poetics and rhetoric discussed formal devices, the *techne* of composition, in a general way, so that the results could be applied to any subject, to any class of thing (Aristotle, *Rhetoric,* bk. I, ch. II, para. 1). They dealt universally with "the ordering and distribution of matter," the "place to which each thing is to be assigned" (Cicero(?), *Ad Herennium,* bk. I, ch. II, para. 3), a major factor that contributed to the paradigmatic way in which these studies on poetics and rhetoric were received and through which all arts developed with a deep consciousness of unity of means and purpose.

Indeed, all classical works, buildings included, have an oratorical or conversational, humanlike tone, as if made out of a "sweet stuff" (Aristotle, *Poetics,* bk. VI, para. 2). Through the introduction of formal devices, they cultivate affectivity, raise interest and even suspense. As a result, these works have been adored throughout centuries and continents for their persistance of "balance" and "symmetry," "focus" and "finality," and "proportionality" and "hierarchy"; their divisibility through distinct, elementary, concise themes; and their unity through explicit, computable, standard, generative combinatorial plans, small in number but infinitely flexible and adaptable.

Indeed, what characterizes any work—a tragedy, a musical piece, a temple—put together according to the rules of composition that originated in classical poetics and rhetoric is its identity as something "complete and whole," "perfect," whose particular order sets it off from its surroundings (Aristotle, *Poetics,* ch. VII, para. 2–4). It is, again, like an "organism," distinct from its environment because of its internal constitution and the strong demarcation of its limits (ibid.). Every classical work is, in a sense, a temenos, cut out from the rest of the universe by virtue of its special order. To fashion this work is to make a world within the world.

The purpose of this worldmaking, to use a term coined by the philosopher Nelson Goodman (1981), is to "instruct and persuade" according to the classical rhetoricians (Aristotle, *The Art of Rhetoric,* bk. 1, ch. 2, para. 1), to "purge," that is, carry out a "catharsis" of the emotions (Aristotle, *Poetics,* ch. VI, para. 2). The work should affect the minds of the audience for the sake of public good. It should edify wisely, consult and comment judiciously, defend and praise, rouse consciousness, and criticize. Thus worldmaking, as it applies to classical works of art, in the words of another ancient rhetorician, Hermagoras, is *politicón*—it is political.

In addition to these writings on poetics and rhetoric, one has to investigate the architectural texts by Vitruvius's commentators, the other "trattatisti" and theoreticians of classical architecture, and the illustrations of architecture presented in these treatises. Although illustrations do not supply formal categories manifestly, they do imply them, especially when representations are accompanied by justification or explanatory diagrams, as they operate in an intermediate plane between verbal abstraction and concrete object. For this reason they are most valuable instruments of formal analysis.

A final source to draw from is the formal study of other arts, such as music, poetry, and oratory. Since the time of Lessing's seminal work, *Laocoon* (1766), which compared poetry with the visual arts, many studies have been carried out to identify the structural parallels and contrasts among different artistic media that aspire to the classical view of composition.

It is not inconceivable that such formal parallels reflect common cognitive structures, a system of rules that constitute language or music competence as well as architecture and that these rules all stem from a common ground or run parallel to each other. A rushed use of key words such as "language," "syntax," "grammar" has been made, following this hypothesis, leading mostly to the familiar "linguistic analogies," as Peter Collins called them (1965, p. 173). But these are only speculations that require in-depth investigation and testing. And the time has not yet come for such claims to be proven.

Setting aside the task of researching deeper foundations of thinking to explain classical architecture, we turn to the study of the middle-range rules, what we have called the poetics of classical architecture, the canonic system of formal conventions, shaped through history and borne on the top of innate mental structures.

The canonic system that operates when a classical building is being composed or appreciated, we shall argue in the next pages of this book, can be summarized through three levels of formal devices: (1) *Taxis,* which divides architectural works into parts; (2) *genera,* the individual elements that populate the parts as divided by taxis; and (3) *symmetry,* the relations between individual elements.

The three levels of the canon that make up the poetics of classical architecture are equally important and operate simultaneously in shaping a building. In addition, they are proscriptive, not prescriptive. This means that they do not so much direct action as *constrain* it, to use a notion mostly associated with the fields of artificial intelligence and linguistics (see Halle and Keyser 1981; Marr 1982; and Berwick 1985). In other words, instead of telling us what to do, they tell us what not to. This may seem to be a subtle equivocation. But it explains why so many new classical formal arrangements have been, are, and probably will continue to be created out of the same canon. By constraining rather than directing, the classical canon allows for a certain degree of freedom and invention in responding to those forces of change that lie outside the world of forms.

We now turn to the study of the three levels of the classical canon.

I RULES OF COMPOSITION

1 Taxis: The Framework

In the *Poetics* of Aristotle, as we have already observed, the work of art is a world within the world, "complete," "integral," "whole," a world where there is no contradiction. Noncontradiction is ensured through the functioning of three levels of formal organization. The first is what Aristotle called *taxis,* the orderly arrangement of parts (*Poetics,* bk. VII, para. 35). It will be dealt with here. The other two, the *genera* and *symmetry,* are the subjects of the next two chapters.

Taxis divides a building into parts and fits into the resulting partitions the architectural elements, producing a coherent work. In other words, taxis constrains the placing of the architectural elements that populate a building by establishing successions of logically organized divisions of space.

Taxis contains two sublevels, which we will call *schemata:* the *grid* and the *tripartition.* The grid schema divides the building through two sets of lines. In the *rectangular* grid schema, which is the one most commonly used in classical architecture, straight lines meet at right angles. The distance between these lines is often equal, cutting the composition into equal parts. In cases when the distances between these lines are not equal, they alter regularly (see figure 2). In both cases, the composition is sectioned into parts that vary in a coherent way (see figure 3). There is also a *polar* grid schema, which also sections the building coherently. We talk about it later. The grid schema (see figure 4) can be expanded by substituting planes for the lines. The planes

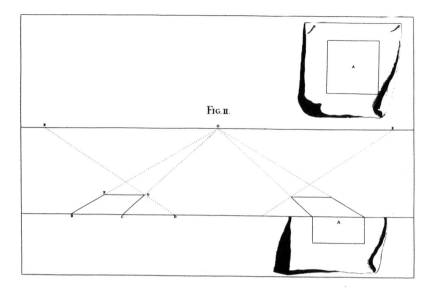

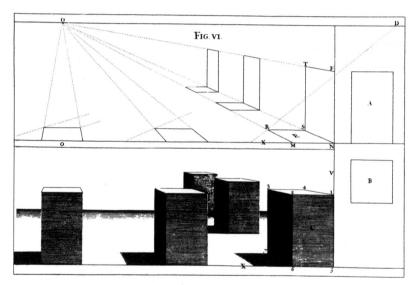

1. Pozzo (1693–1700).

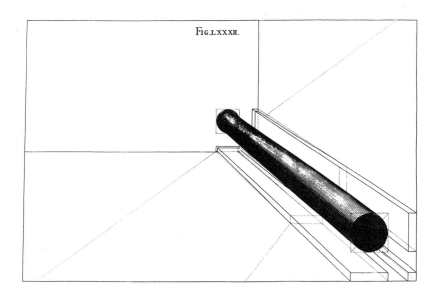

Fig. LXXXII.

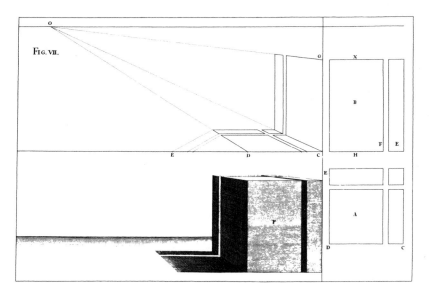

Fig. VII.

2. Rectangular grid schemata sectioning a composition equally (Serlio 1619).

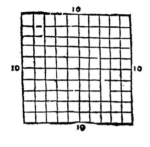

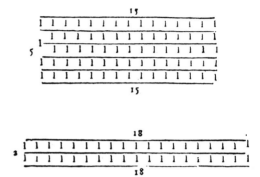

3. Rectangular grid schema subdividing a composition into regular parts of varying size (Cousin 1560).

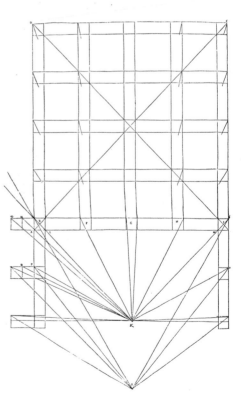

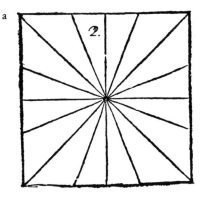

a

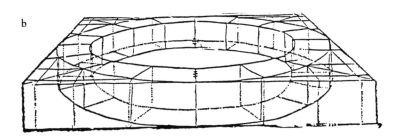

b

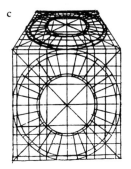

c

4. Polar grid patterns. (a, b) Serlio
(1619). (c) Du Cerceau (1576).

function in a similar manner as the lines, partitioning space and controlling the position of the architectural element (see figures 5–7).

A building made out of a single homogeneous division (a), runs no risk of violating taxis. Metaphorically, we might call it a tautology. It is itself; it contains no element that can contradict it. It can be pictured as an undivided cube. This initial form pattern has for centuries fascinated architects who espouse classicism as the par excellence coherent division schema. It can justifiably be seen, however, as trivial in its simple single-mindedness, as it has many times in history.

A form pattern, which might be perceived as a little more complex and rich, is generated by dividing the initial unit of the cube into equal minicubic parts (see figures 5, 6, 17) or else by multiplying the initial cube into a larger cubic unit (see figures 5, 17). In both cases the result is the same: a work that contains no contradictory ways of partitioning. This kind of *grid pattern* is illustrated in the following diagram:

$$
\begin{array}{ccccccccc}
 & & & a & & a & & a & \\
 & & a & & a & & a & & a \\
 & a & & a & & a & & a & \\
a & & a & & a & & a & & a \\
a & & a & & a & & a^{a} & & a \\
a & & a & & a & & a^{a} & & \\
a & & a & & a & & a^{a} & & \\
a & & a & & a & & a & &
\end{array}
$$

This formal taxis, or pattern, with its obsessive consistency, is one of the means of making the world orderly, set apart from the rest of the universe where anything goes. The classical overriding norms of "completeness," "integrality," and "wholeness" are also enforced by tripartition.

The schema of *tripartition* marks the difference between the internal and external sections of a work. It divides a building into three parts, two border parts and one enclosed. The "whole," states Aristotle, is tripartite: It has "a beginning, a middle and an end" (*Poetics*, ch. VII, para. 35). The idea of closed composition and the formal condition of a "border" part certainly hold memories of the well-guarded territory of the temenos. But already in the *Poetics* of Aristotle, tripartition is deprived of any divinatory connotation.

In classical architecture the beginning and the end can be equivalent, bilaterally symmetrical. Contrary to tragedy or music, architecture is seen most frequently in a reversible way. One can return to the end part of a building and make it read as the beginning; one looks at a building from right to left and vice versa. The same convention does not apply,

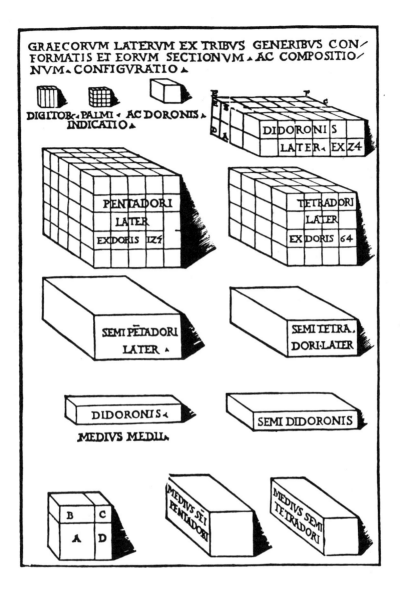

GRAECORVM LATERVM EX TRIBVS GENERIBVS CON⁄
FORMATIS ET EORVM SECTIONVM ⬤ AC COMPOSITIO⁄
NVM⬤ CONFIGVRATIO ▲

DIGITOB⬤ PALMI ⬤ AC DORONIS ▲
INDICATIO ▲

DIDORONIS
LATER⬤ EX Z4

PENTADORI
LATER
EX DORIS IZ⁵

TETRADORI
LATER
EX DORIS 64

SEMI PENTADORI
LATER ▲

SEMI TETRA⬤
DORI·LATER

DIDORONIS ⬤
MEDIVS MEDII⬤

SEMI DIDORONIS

B C
A D

MEDIVS SEI
PENTADORI

MEDIVS SEMI
TETRADORI

5. Three-dimensional grid patterns
(Cesariano 1521).

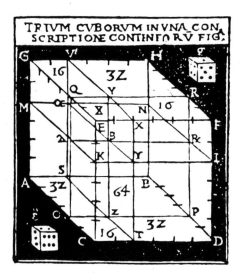

TRIVM CVBORVM IN VNA CON SCRIPTIONE CONTINTO RV FIG.

6. Three-dimensional grid patterns
(Cesariano 1521).

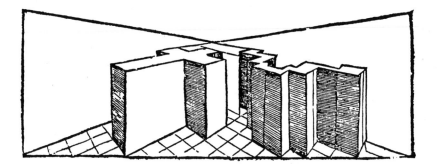

7. Designs following rectangular
grid schemata (Serlio 1619).

8. Designs following rectangular
grid schemata (Serlio 1619).

9. Designs following rectangular
grid schemata (Rusconi 1590).

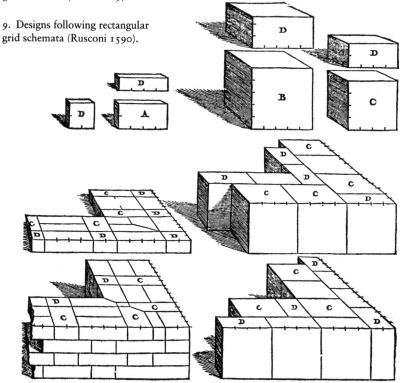

however, to the top and bottom parts. They are not accepted as equivalent; their arrangement is not reversible.

The tripartite schema divides façade, plan, and section of a building into three major parts. Moreover, it can be applied again to segment further each of these parts in the same fashion. The operation can be repeated, the tripartite schema creating at each step a coherent nested relation among parts and between parts and whole. In general, taxis, whether in its overall grid schema or tripartition, should be seen as applied *hierarchically* from the whole to the part, one grid or tripartition schema *embedded* in another. In fact, this hierarchical correspondence among divisions in applying taxis schemata from the general to the particular, from the total to the last detail, is also a means through which the norm of noncontradiction is respected. Hence the legend that in a classical work, even if only a tiny fragment survives, one can always reconstruct the whole.

Let us now look at taxis and its formal schemata as they are illustrated in theoretical work on classical architecture and as they have been applied diagrammatically in specific buildings.

Taxis is a key category in Vitruvius's *De Architectura*. Here, *taxis* is defined as the "balanced adjustment of the details of a work separately, and, as to the whole, the arrangement of the proportion with a view to a symmetrical result" (bk. I, ch. II, para. 2). Compared with Aristotle's, this definition is not very clear. However, what is clear is how Vitruvius applies taxis in practice. Tripartition, for example, underlies Vitruvius's classification of temples (bk. III, ch. II). The first kind of temple is "in antis," which in Greek is called "naos en parastasin." The second is the prostyle. Both are distinguished by having a front part (*pronaos*) attached to their main unarticulated, uniformal volume, the *naos* or *cella*. This front part consists of pilasters (a kind of column engaged to the wall) or of columns standing in a free row, forming what is called a *portico*, a porch. The third kind of temple in the Vitruvian classification is the "amphiprostyle," which has columns in both (*amphi-*) front and back parts, in other words a portico at each end. The back part is called *opisthodomus*, back building. Last is the "peripteral" temple, which has columns all around (*peri-*). The initial unitary volume is separated not only into a front and back part but also on the two sides. With the latter, we finally arrive at a plan of a building that is divided in three from every view. The tripartite taxis is completely satisfied. All the other temples we have just seen can be considered as deriving from this tripartite type.

Let us put these three kinds of temples in a *formula* made of letters, each letter standing for an architectural part. This might seem an unnecessarily esoteric way of describing a building, but its usefulness will become clear in the next step of our study of taxis.

Here is how these formulas might look:

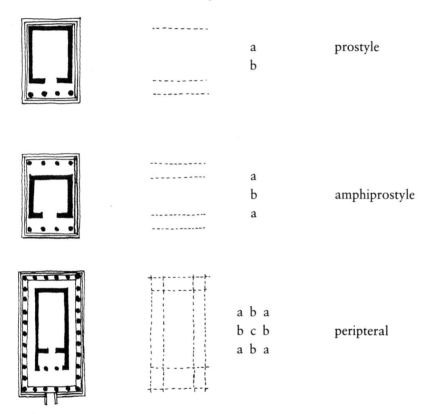

a	prostyle
b	

a	
b	amphiprostyle
a	

a b a	
b c b	peripteral
a b a	

Vitruvius provides more kinds of temples—*pseudodipteros, dipteros, hypaethral*—adding parts and/or rows of columns or *deleting* them. All these kinds of temples can be derived from the above taxonomy, using the same logic of partitioning, the same formula of tripartition.

What is interesting in Vitruvius's catalogue of temples is not so much his "typology" of buildings but his *system* of classification. This system contained an implicit method for generating plans, an architectural *ars combinatoria* developed by sectioning an initial corpus associated with the tripartite schema. It was a way of looking at buildings that became fundamental in classical architecture.

Now let us see how the commentators of Vitruvius prolonged and further explored his system of classification. The illustrations of Cesariano's 1521 edition of *De Architectura* are of the greatest importance for shaping the canon of classical architecture as based on the ideas and works of antiquity. Cesariano was a painter, a scholar, and an architect. His edition of Vitruvius's work is highly significant for students of classical architecture because of the success it had at its time and the prestige it carried. It expressed the ideas of its period and influenced those to come. It was the first translation of Vitruvius in vernacular Italian to be printed; it was illustrated amply and contained a most extensive verbal commentary. Both schemas of taxis, the grid and tripartition, are present in the series of illustrations to Vitruvius's third book.

The grid is stated in a nonspecific, general manner covering the whole area of the building (see figure 10). It is also applied in a specific way, its vertical and horizontal lines controlling the position of the walls of the church, defining the area for the nave and the aisle. The grid is made of unequal units or of identical square ones (see figures 11–13). More specifically, we can follow one of Cesariano's examples and see how a square grid is applied (see figure 11). It segments the plan into the following seven parts:

A B C D C B A.

The middle unit, D, is sectioned into two identical B units (notice that we are following Cesariano's own notations closely). The whole now reads

A B C B B C B A.

The plan contains the basic classical tripartite schema. There is a beginning part B, engaged between parts A and C. There is a middle part BB between parts C and C, and there is an end part A that is identical with the initial one. We condense Cesariano's notation in order to point out the presence of the tripartite schema as follows:

A B C B B C B A   into   a b a.

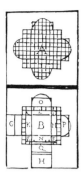

10. Grid pattern (Cesariano 1521).

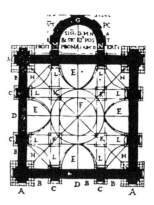

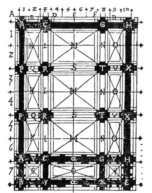

11. Grid pattern (Cesariano 1521).

12. Grid patterns (Cesariano 1521).

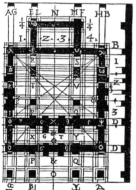

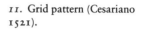

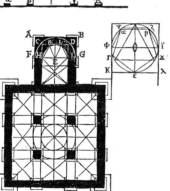

13. Grid patterns (Serlio 1619).

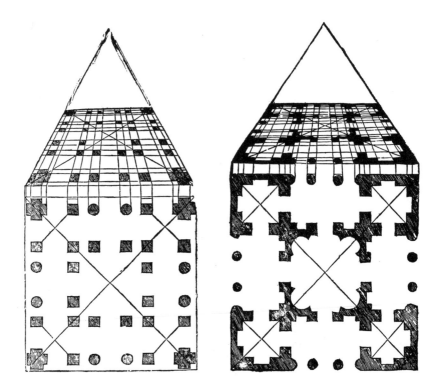

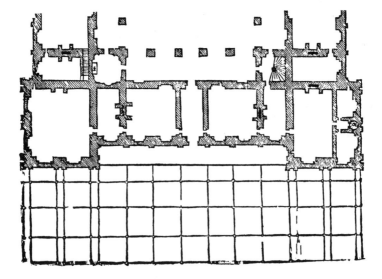

We can transcribe Cesariano's plan in its entirety with his notation adding only the X letter where no notation is already provided.

```
A  B  C  D  C  B  A
B  H  L  E  L  H  B
C  L  K  X  K  L  C
D  E  X  F  X  E  D .
C  L  K  X  K  L  C
B  H  L  E  L  H  B
A  B  C  D  C  B  A
```

As a next step, we can rewrite the plan pattern, simplifying it to demonstrate, as we did before, its tripartite organization. The result is

```
a   b   a
b   c   b  .
a   b   a
```

Here we find the Aristotelian tripartite schema expressed in the most elementary way. We also find again the Vitruvian temple formula. This "square and cross," as this pattern has been called, has been one of the most predominant formal patterns of classical architecture since the Renaissance. For this reason we call it the mother taxis formula.

Let us now slightly expand the formula by inserting between the end and the middle main parts an intermediary part. This permits us to demonstrate the workings of the combinatorics of classical architecture and to relate the formula more easily to specific buildings.

```
a   b   c   b   a
b   c   d   c   b
c   d   f   d   c
b   c   d   c   b
a   b   c   b   a
```

We now apply some simple operations to the formula, such as deletion of parts, fusion of parts, addition of parts, and substitution of parts by hierarchically embedding other parts and finally translating the rectangular grid into a polar one. The mother formula can be transformed into a number of taxis patterns by the following operations:

1. deletion of parts

```
        c          b c b       a b c b a     a b c b a
     e d e       b   d   b     b       b     b       b    a b c b a
   c d f d c     c d f d c     c         c   c   f   c    c d f d c
     e d e       b   d   b     b       b     b       b    b c d c b
        c          b c b       a b c b a     a b c b a    a b c b a
```

2. fusion of parts

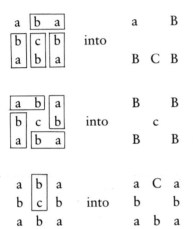

```
   a  b  a                a      B

   b  c  b     into

   a  b  a                B  C  B
```

```
   a  b  a               B      B

   b  c  b     into          c

   a  b  a               B      B
```

```
   a  b  a               a  C  a

   b  c  b     into       b     b

   a  b  a               a  b  a
```

3. addition or repetition of parts

```
a b c b a
b c d c b
c d f d c
b c d c b
b c d c b
a b c b a
```

4. embedding of parts

```
                          d e d         d e d
                          e f e    b    e f e
                          d e d         d e d

   a b a
   b c b     into           b       c     b
   a b a

                            a       b     a
```

It might be interesting to look now at a number of plans of classical architecture to see, without much detailed analysis, how closely they come to these plan patterns. In the five taxis patterns by Serlio, for example, which follow here, "simple" means that the *ars combinatoria* of classical architecture are at work. They, like other taxis patterns by Serlio (see figures 108, 109), offer countless options rather than a monotonous repetition of a single idea.

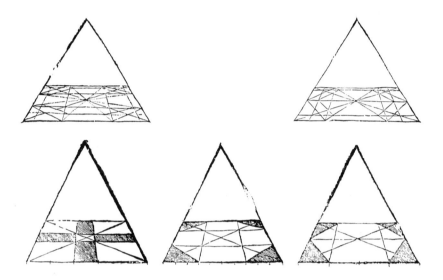

It is clear that these departures from the mother formula must, as an effect, underline its generative potentials, rather than subvert its constraining rule.

Another taxis pattern from the mother formula is the *polar* one, which we mentioned earlier, found in *tholoi, rotondae,* or other circular buildings. Both the grid and the tripartite schemata are present here, but the grid schema, instead of being *rectangular* as in the cases examined, is *polar*. One set of dividing lines forms concentric circles, while the other radiates from the common center of these circles. The tripartite schema is present but in a kind of *perpetuum mobile,* running in a circular manner. From the viewpoint of spatial logic, such polar patterns are derived from the following operation:

5. translation of the Cesariano mother formula

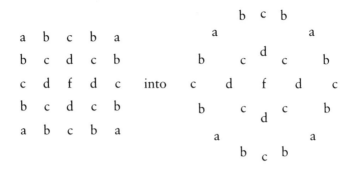

Finally, we have buildings that bring together rectangular formulas and polar ones, creating hybrid formal patterns that integrate grids and tripartition schemata, for example, Saint Peter in Rome (see figure 111) and Saint Peter in Montorio by Bramante (see figure 113). Renaissance architects were quite fond of such compositions based on hybrid patterns.

One should not get the impression from these examples that taxis applies only to the overall parts of a building. On the contrary, it is applicable to the smallest detail. This is demonstrated more systematically in the next chapter, when the genera of architecture are discussed.

Taxis and its schemata are applied to buildings, regardless of their use. Churches, palaces, villas, gardens, and town plans can adopt the same plan pattern. The so-called centralized cross pattern, even more the formal schemata from which it was derived, is not the property of a specific architect's work. Wittkower's table of "Schematized plans of eleven of Palladio's villas" (1949), which has triggered so many interesting discussions on typology in architecture, although not incorrect in its application to Palladio's work, has had many misleading implications. It has obscured the fact that taxis and its schemata are general ordering devices and that their roots in the system of thought of classical poetics go beyond neoplatonism.

The presence of the same taxis frame in artifacts of different meanings and uses is characteristic, in fact, of other cultural expressions that have adopted the classical canon: poetry, painting, and especially music. Ecclesiastical or operatic music, a dance, or a piece of chamber music can have the same musical subdivisions, the same formal schemata of partitioning. The compliance with the classical canon implies the introduction of normative schemata, with their combinations and transformations close to those used in classical architecture. The tripartition schema is present in all formal expressions of classical art. All classical works, whether in words, sounds, or shapes, are identifiable by their strict adherence to the schema that demarcates a realm of departure, a central realm, and a realm of arrival. It comes under many names: opening, continuation, completion; introduction, main part, conclusion; exposition, development, recapitulation. Most typical are the sonata form (Momigny 1806) and the ABA rondo form in music, in which the melodic strings are structured in rise (*monte*), bridge (*ponte*), and descent (*fonte*) parts (Ratner 1980, pp. 39, 213). As in architecture and literature, so in music, the length of each part is unimportant. What matters is the clear distinction of each section, the characteristic formal role it plays, and the rigorous application of the principle at every interlocked hierarchical step of the work. Riemann's (1903) eight-measure period (or eight-measure phrase pattern) rendition analysis in classical music (*Vierhebigkeit*), an exaggerated but operational musical structuring device, resembles the analysis of classical architectural taxis in many respects. As in classical music, so in architecture, taxis acts not so much through the duplication of formulas as through new combinatorial formal patterns. There are other similarities in the application of taxis to the arts. The ABCDCBA taxis spatial formula encountered in Cesariano's illustrations is close to the crisscross pattern often found in classical poetry and rhetoric, known as the *chiasmus* pattern, and in its ABCBBCBA version it resembles the *octave* or *octet* form of the classical sonnet of the Renaissance.

Musical, textual, and architectural phrasing, periodization, and sectioning reflect classical taxis. For some psychologists this leads to speculations about the structure of the mind. Without disputing the search of cognitive science for fundamental laws of thinking—which to us lie much deeper than the formal frames referred to here—we suggest that the explanation is probably historical. The canon of all cultural expressions of the Renaissance has been put together as a convention in accordance with the same paradigms supplied by Aristotle, Vitruvius, and buildings of antiquity.

A final point concerning how we can represent graphically the sections of taxis on a building. From the Renaissance on, taxis and its normative schemata have controlled an architectural composition by setting up contours, regulatory lines or planes, that plot limits defining the parts within which the individual architectural elements lie (see figure 14). Toward the nineteenth century another way of specifying the divisions of a work became dominant: specification by an axis rather than by an outline. It is presupposed here that the architectural members of the section indicated by the axis are laid out—"balanced"— around the axis according to bilateral symmetry (see figure 15). A comparison of the Cesariano diagrams (1521; see figure 12) and those from Durand's *Précis* (1802; see figure 18) is rather revealing. Occasionally both methods seem to be mixed, as several perspective studies seem to imply, such as in the case of Cousin's *Livre de perspective* (see figure 16).

The shift from contour to axis by the beginning of the nineteenth century was probably due to the increasing scientific nature of architecture, the use of the bilateral symmetry axis being widespread at the time in such avant-garde fields as statics, crystallography, and the morphology of plants and animals. It marks a step toward abstraction, and it facilitates the application of multiple taxis formulas on the same object, one laid over the other, as Guadet's illustration demonstrates (see figure 15).

As classical architecture became a less favorable idiom and as the classical canon came to be seen as a despised formal straitjacket, it was taxis and its schemata that were first and most viciously attacked. The picturesque, romantic, regionalist, expressionist, and modernist anti-classicism took shape only after an alternative to the classical taxis of grid structures and tripartition was devised.

Taxis has a special place in the classical poetics of architecture. Swans and dolphins, garlands, wings and torches, scrolls and sphinxes might crumble, but taxis will remain. Mario Praz imagined Winckelmann, one of the greatest proponents of classical architecture in history, "in the gloomy realms of Hades . . . holding in his arms the winged genius, . . . the loveliest of all figures, . . . wandering thus, ecstatically and smiling through the meadows" (Praz 1969). It is possible that if one could come closer to Winckelmann's shadow, one would recognize him holding just a plain frame, his most beloved perfect order of divisions.

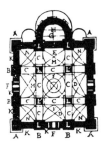

14. Alternative grid pattern notation systems (Serlio 1619).

15. Alternative grid pattern notation system (Guadet 1901–1904).

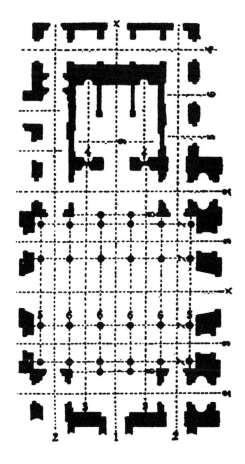

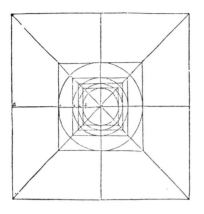
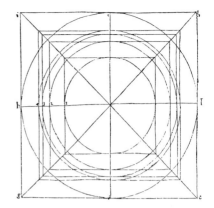

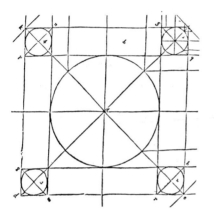

16. Taxis schemata partitioning plans by means of contour and axis (Cousin 1560).

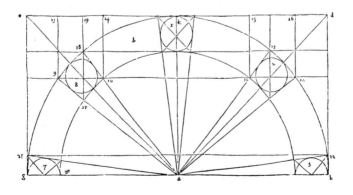

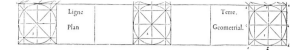

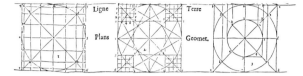

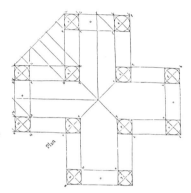

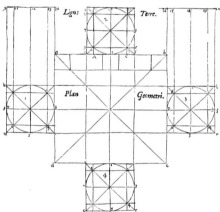

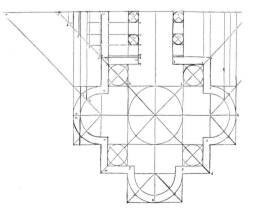

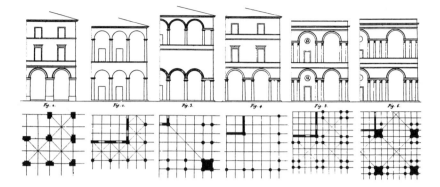

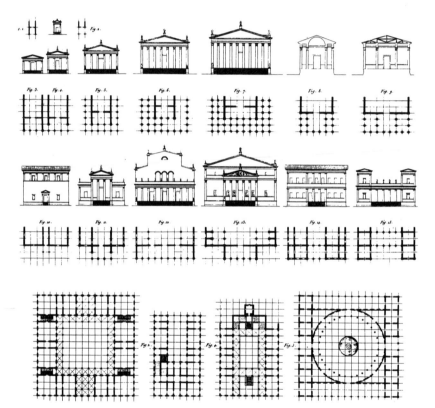

17. Taxis schemata sectioning plans by means of the axis (Durand 1802–1805).

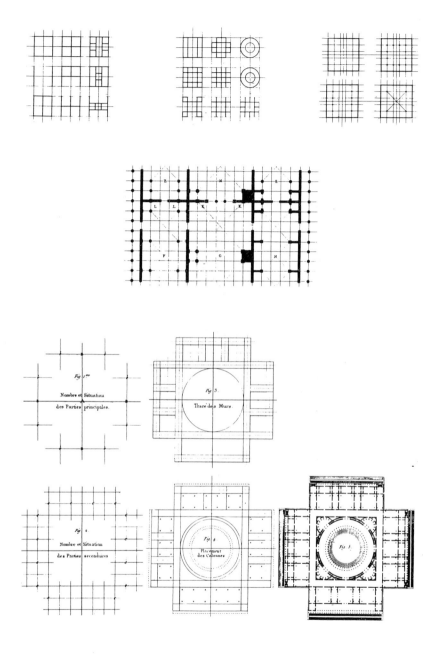

18. Alternative taxis schemata.
Plans with subdivisions of plans
embedded in them. From Durand
(1802–1805).

2 The Genera: The Elements

Once an architectural composition has been ordered by taxis, once it has been laid out (that is, sectioned and subsectioned), then it is ready to be occupied, populated if you will, by architectural elements. One of the most intriguing aspects of classical architecture is that these elements always appear in well-determined sets governed by particular fixed relations. This level of the formal canon of classical architecture is usually referred to as the classical orders. But *orders* is a misleading term. It implies that there is only one means of ordering a building, only one principle at work in the classical poetics of order. In reality, orders are only one of three—the others being taxis and symmetry, which is the subject of the next chapter.

For the sake of argument, then, let us adopt instead of orders the term *genera,* from the Latin *genus, generis* meaning origin, race, species. Vitruvius used it. So did many architectural writers in the classical tradition. Serlio, for example, echoed the Vitruvian text literally when he referred to the *generatione* (1619, bk. IV). As late as the seventeenth century, we find *espèces,* in Claude Perrault's *Ordonnance des cinq espèces de colonne* (Paris, 1683). And, indeed, *genus* is a good word for expressing the idea of typified, predetermining relations that bind together the members of certain groups.

In comparison with taxis and symmetry, the genera have received a disproportionately large amount of attention. The differences in interpretation have also been great. Vitruvius, for one, viewed the genera as products of concrete circumstances, as entities born at specific moments under characteristic conditions. The Doric genus, he claimed, took its name from the type of temple first built by Dorus and dedicated to Juno in the city of Argos (Vitruvius, *De Architectura*, bk. IV, ch. I); the Ionic genus assumed its name "because the Ionians made it first"; as for the Corinthian, it was equally tied to a certain time and place. On the grave of a Corinthian girl a basket was left on the root of an acanthus, forcing its shoots to grow out at the sides, curve downward, and then curl into volutes. Callimachos, an architect, passed by the object and, pleased by the effect, modeled the Corinthian capital on its example.

This profane approach reveals the influence of the same Lucretian materialism to be seen in many other parts of Vitruvius's work, an influence that late Renaissance and Counter-Reformation architects tried to obscure, associating Vitruvian theory exclusively with neoplatonistic mysticism. These authors considered the genera as belonging to a sacred taxonomy, as eternal, absolute, and inviolable limits and boundaries imposed by a divinely ordained *ordo rerum*.

There is a vast list of writings based on the premise of the sacred origins of the genera, their relation to the Temple of Solomon, for example, and to other heavenly prototypes, and their function as a kind of sacred alphabet, beyond human time and place. Such beliefs permeate Cesariano's commentary (1521) on Vitruvius and, to a great extent, the writings of Spanish theoreticians of architecture, especially those influenced by the Counter-Reformation. The most important of the latter is Villalpando's *Ezechielem Explanationes* (1596–1604). In this book, Vitruvius's ideas are systematically merged with doctrines of the Catholic church and with biblical references, especially from the book of Ezekiel.

Of course, some traces of the divinatory thinking do appear in Vitruvius, in particular in his treatment of what he called *decor* (*De Architectura*, bk. I, ch. II, para. 4). This notion, he suggests, dictates which genus is appropriate to the cult of particular deities: the Doric for Minerva, Mars, and Hercules; the Ionic for Juno, Diana, and Bacchus; the Corinthian for Venus, Flora, Prosperine, and the Nymphs. Here, with the genera employed as a means of classification, the link with an archaic past is obvious. Through their role as decor, the genera become what Lévi-Strauss (1966, ch. I *passim*) would have called a "science of the concrete," partitioning the world through anthropomorphic categories of sex (males versus female) and age (young versus old) and expressing these differences through symbolic spatial architectural relations. Hence the proportions of the members of the temple must resemble those of a "hominis bene figurati membrorum" (*De Architectura,* bk. III, ch. I, para. 1), the members of a well-formed human body. Vitruvius here is certainly prerational. He goes so far as to claim that the sections of the column—the capital, the shaft, and the base—are derived from the main divisions of the human body—the head, the body, and the feet (*De Architectura,* bk. III, para. 1).

In the writings of the Renaissance, this anthropomorphic aspect of classical architecture frequently becomes, one might say, eroticized, the object of carnal desire. Poliphilo, the hero of the *Hypnerotomachia Poliphili* by Francesco Colonna, is infatuated with the proportions of the portal of a temple because they remind him of his beloved, Polia. Consumed with passion, he is irresistibly drawn to penetrate, as he says, the orifice (p. ciiii). More recently, Paul Valéry (1921) places into the architect Eupalinos's mouth the following declaration:

Unbeknownst to all, this delicate temple is the mathematical image of a young maiden of Corinth whom I once sweetly loved. It faithfully reproduces her particular proportions. It feels alive to me.

A certain degree of erotic content can be read into the very names, clearly of anthropomorphic origin, of some of the members of the genera. The concrete forms of the genera themselves might appear no less suggestive: the thickening and the thinning of the fleshlike little waves of matter on a Lesbian cymation; the shallowly grooved cylinders of the columns; the gently curved *ovolo* and *apophyge,* swollen as if by smooth caressing. Indeed, if one leans against a column on a summer afternoon, it really can make the heart quiver, the skin tighten, the cheeks flush, breathing quicken.

Of course, there are those who do not share a sense of wonder and delight on beholding the classical genera, who feel completely alien and indifferent to them, who find their intricate articulations and configurations an enormous bore. This seems to imply that the attachment to classical architecture, far from being an instinctual response, is an acquired taste, a matter of adopting or rejecting conventions and cultural values established at a certain moment in history and in a given social context.

There was also a wholly different approach to the antique genera, an attempt to Christianize them. During the late Renaissance, Serlio

(1537), after having increased the Vitruvian canon of the four genera—Doric, Ionic, Corinthian, and Tuscan—to five with the addition of the Composite order (see figure 19), also updated the Vitruvian notion of decor, by relating each of the antique pagan genera to the divine personae of Christianity. He maintained that, as the ancients had reserved the Doric for temples to Jupiter, Mars, and Hercules, so architects of his own times should dedicate Doric churches to Christ the Redemptor; Saint Paul or Saint George, who possessed the same kind of virility; and their ancient predecessors (Serlio 1619, ch. IV, proemio and para. 6). In a similar vein he wished to transpose the Corinthian to monasteries and cloisters devoted to the cult of the Virgin in order to impart to them the connotation of virtue and chastity, which it had acquired in antiquity (Serlio 1619, ch. IV, para. 1).

Serlio also tried to modernize classical architecture in another, more secular sense. Observing a world increasingly characterized by instability, mobility, and class conflict, he called for the social rank and profession of the owners of private buildings and public buildings to be reflected in the robustness or delicacy of the genus (Serlio 1619). Vitruvius had already suggested this social ranking (*De Architectura*, bk. VI, para. 5). For Serlio, it is the fundamental raison d'être of the orders (Serlio 1619, ch. IV, "Ai lettori"). The same happened to music. In the absolutist court culture, the key system was also employed to express social hierarchy (Ratner 1980; Riepel 1755). The key of C became the symbolic register of the landowner, F of the day laborer, just as the Corinthian genus in architecture identified the prince, and the Tuscan, the soldier. Of course, the relation among architectural good manners, decorum, and social felicity were infinitely more complex, especially given the active public life of the elegant society, with its continuous acting out of the structure of power in order to hammer home dependencies and obligations.

The genera also became the object of rigorous mathematical theorizing. In the Renaissance it was widely taken for granted that there existed invariant ways of calculating the proportions of the genera. Much effort went into working out theoretical support for the universality of architectural proportions on the grounds that they corresponded to the laws of nature. Consistent as these pronouncements were with the currently prestigious wave of neoplatonism, they ultimately failed to yield anything but conjecture. In a more empirical vein, Fréart de Chambray, in his *Parallèle de l'architecture antique et de la moderne* (1659), tried to compare systematically both ancient and modern buildings that were accepted at that time as canonical and, thus, to reveal proportionality constants of beauty. The trouble was that his evidence was not reliable. The publication in 1682 of Antoine Desgodetz's *Edifices antiques de Rome* redeemed this weakness. The book consisted of a series of detailed and accurate measured drawings of the remains of the ancient Roman monuments—the first such series in history—carried out under the sponsorship of the Académie Royale d'Architecture in Paris. The empirical evidence was overwhelmingly conclusive: Far from being absolute norms, the ancient Roman architectural proportions varied with every building.

The full implication of these findings were brought out not by Desgodetz, who provided but a scanty text to accompany his drawings, but by Claude Perrault (Tzonis 1972; Hermann 1973) also in the service of the Académie. He argued that the proportions of buildings of equal beauty were variant. But, in addition, he concluded that beauty itself resided not in the object beheld but in the relation of this object with power of the owner.

Of course, there had been a small number of theoreticians who had postulated, even before Desgodetz and Perrault had carried out their definite demonstration, that the genera were not invariant, sacred, or natural categories and that their design was mainly the result of convention. Their reaction was to assume that designers should be able to give free reign to their inventiveness. This position was welcomed in those courts that relied on nationalist support and that found expressions of cultural independence congenial. Architecte du Roi Philibert de l'Orme's project for a sixth, French order in the *Premier tôme d'architecture* of 1567 (p. 219) found favor in the court of the Valois. This was the first major attempt in history to supplement the list of five genera based on antique prototypes—Doric, Ionic, Corinthian, Tuscan, and Composite—through the invention of a wholly new one.

Equally unorthodox were Perrault's own proposal for a French order in the 1670s, that of Pierre Cottart in his *Recueil des oeuvres* (1671), of Sebastien le Clerc in his *Traité d'architecture* (1714, II, pl. 177, 178), of Charles-Augustin d'Aviler in his *Cours d'architecture* (1691, pl. 89), and of Roland le Virloys in his *Dictionnaire* (1770, pl. 19). Ribart de Chamoust devoted a whole book to *l'Ordre français trouvé dans la*

b

19. Two series on columnar elements: (a) on pedestals, (b) on bases. Both are ranked from the Tuscan to the Composite (Serlio 1619).

nature (1776) to support his proposal for a new order, which was more relevant to the growing rigorist movement of the time than to the classical canon. There were also other proposals, such as le Clerc's for a Spanish order, L. C. Sturm's for a German one (1699) and James Adam's (1762) for a British one. H. Emlyn's proposal was extensively developed in his *Proposition of a New Order in Architecture* as late as 1797.

An altogether different approach, of a functionalist inclination, interpreted the genera as a sort of iconography of construction, as diagrams visualizing the way horizontal loads in a building are transmitted to the ground. Typical of this approach were Schopenhauer's writings on architecture. The German romantic philosopher argued that the "proper theme" or architecture was "gravity, rigidity and cohesion . . . not, as has been assumed hitherto . . . form, proportion and symmetry" (Schopenhauer 1966). But by seeing genera merely as representations of "support and load," Schopenhauer could explain them only up to a point, dismissing their more essential formal aspects as superfluous, as the result of "playing with the means of art without understanding the ends" (p. 411).

The genera have also been seen as a ranking system. The Tuscan is one extreme of a hierarchy and the Composite, the other, with Doric, Ionic, and Corinthian as in-between points. This ranking has assumed many meanings throughout history, as it is related to history, religion, anthropomorphism, society, and statics. When it comes to discussing the differences between genera, Vitruvius mentions that the origin of the relation between the "thickness of the column" and its height or its size of parts is the human body. The proportions of the Doric column, for example, are derived from the male body. In Vitruvius's words, "whatever thickness they made of the base of the shaft, they raised along with the capital to six times as much in height (*De Architectura,* bk. IV, ch. I, para. 6). This was supposed to express the "strength" and the "grace" of the virile body. The form of the Ionic follows the "feminine slenderness" (*De Architectura,* bk. IV, ch. I, para. 7). "They made the diameter of the column the eighth part of it, so that it might be taller" (*De Architectura,* bk. IV, ch. I, para. 7). In addition to these two modes, the "bare, unadorned and manly" and the "feminine," there is a third, the Corinthian, which "imitates the slight figure of a maiden" (*De Architectura,* bk. IV, ch. I, para. 8).

Like all the interpretations of the genera we have just seen, such a rationalization falls short of explaining the formal obsessions of the classical idiom and its imperative for order, where the genera stand for the *abstract* logical idea of *abstract* ranking and hierarchy, scales of formal modality, if you prefer, of elements that occupy space and that in pragmatic terms can be applied in many different ways. Through this device a building is designed within constraints of proportion and configuration, safe from contradition and from turning into an amorphous compilation. In a similar manner, a composition of classical music is made coherent, distinct from a rumble of noise, by forming a set of sounds of definite pitch and duration. Let us turn now to the genera as such an abstract, formal ranking system to see how this system works. We examine first what is common to all genera, what makes them in fact comparable; then we can see what distinguishes them and accounts for their constituting a scale.

SUBDIVISIONS

Columnar Elements

Remember, in the previous chapter we mentioned that taxis, which refers to subdivision, is applicable to the building as a whole as well as to the smallest detail. Following this, each of the genera is subdivided into three members, and each of these is sectioned once more according to the same rule of tripartition. The genera carry out the classical imperative for order by employing their own particular scheme of tripartition.

In relation to the column, the tripartite division, in descending order, into members is as follows (see figures 19a, 20): (1) the *entablature*, a horizontal member above the column; (2) the *column*, a long vertical cylindrical member; and (3) the *crepidoma* or *stylobate*, a stepped platform on which the column rests, or a *pedestal*, a prismatic member under the column. Each of these members if further divided according to the same schema. As a general rule, tripartition continues to be applied in the same hierarchical manner down to the most basic architectural particle, to the slenderest ripple of matter.

The entablature, then, is articulated into three members (see figures 22, 26, 61): (1) the *cornice*, the uppermost member projecting in the form of a continuous eave; (2) the *frieze*, a band made of blocks resting

20. Doric (a), Ionic (b), and
Corinthian (c) columns with entablatures. From Palladio (1570).

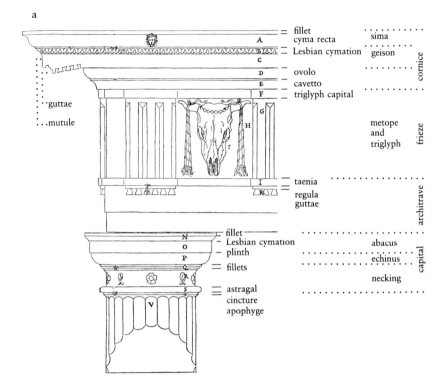

location of
acroterion

a

fillet	
cyma recta	sima
Lesbian cymation	geison
ovolo	
cavetto	cornice
triglyph capital	

guttae

mutule

metope
and
triglyph — frieze

taenia
regula
guttae — architrave

fillet
Lesbian cymation — abacus
plinth — echinus
fillets — capital

necking

astragal
cincture
apophyge

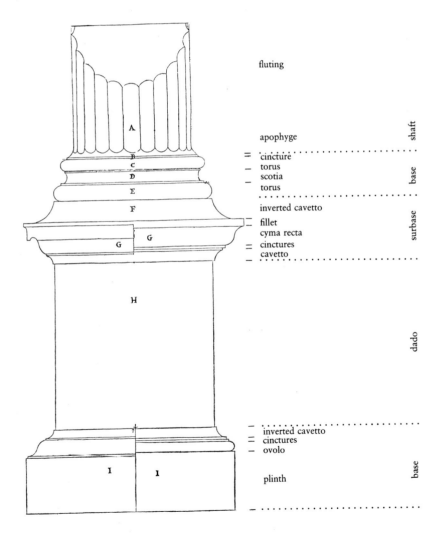

fluting

apophyge .... — shaft

= cincture
— torus
— scotia .... — base
— torus

inverted cavetto
— fillet
cyma recta
= cinctures .... — surbase
— cavetto

dado

— inverted cavetto ....
= cinctures
— ovolo

plinth .... — base

....

b

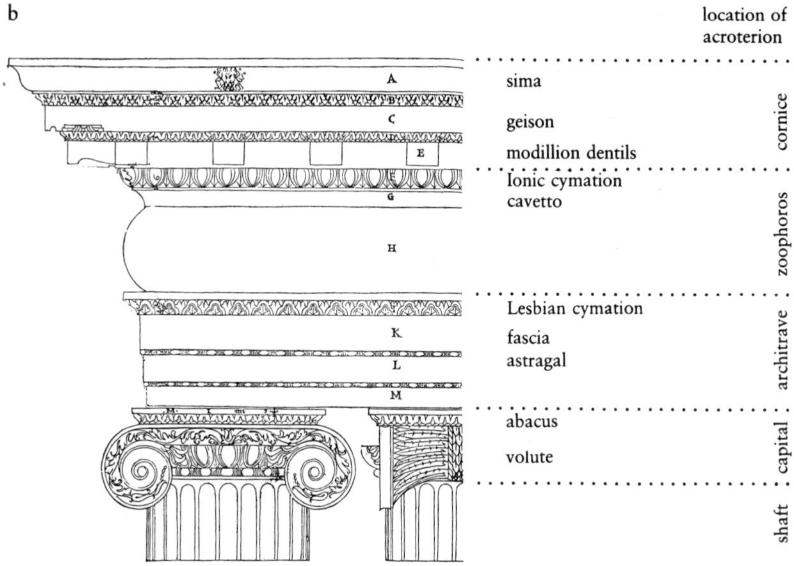

location of
acroterion

sima

geison

modillion dentils

Ionic cymation
cavetto

Lesbian cymation

fascia

astragal

abacus

volute

cornice

zoophoros

architrave

capital

shaft

A

C

E

G

H

K

L

M

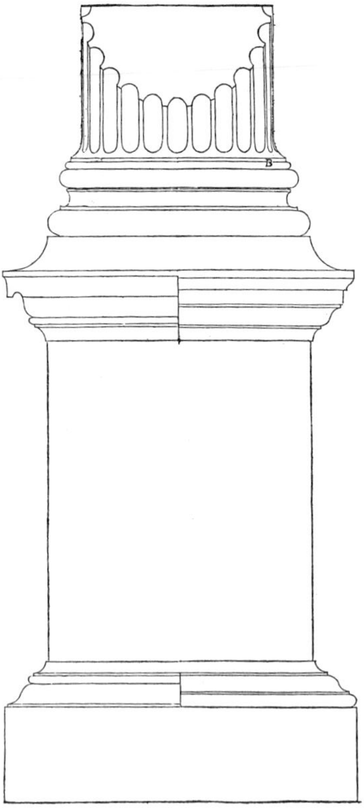

20 *continued*

c

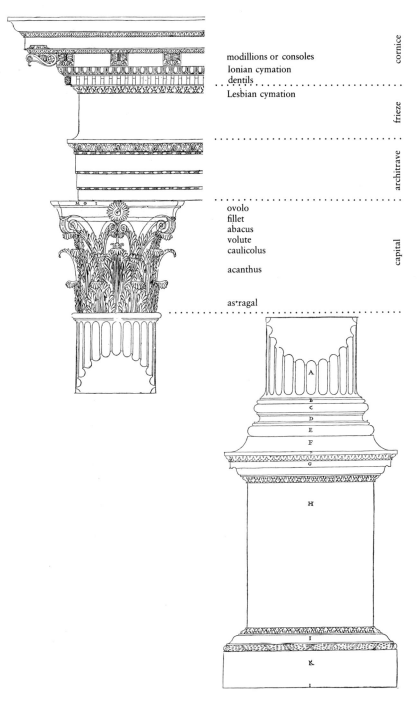

modillions or consoles
Ionian cymation
dentils
Lesbian cymation

ovolo
fillet
abacus
volute
caulicolus

acanthus

astragal

cornice

frieze

architrave

capital

21. Pedestals of the different genera (Scamozzi 1615): (a) Doric, (b) Ionic, (c) Corinthian, (d) Roman.

a

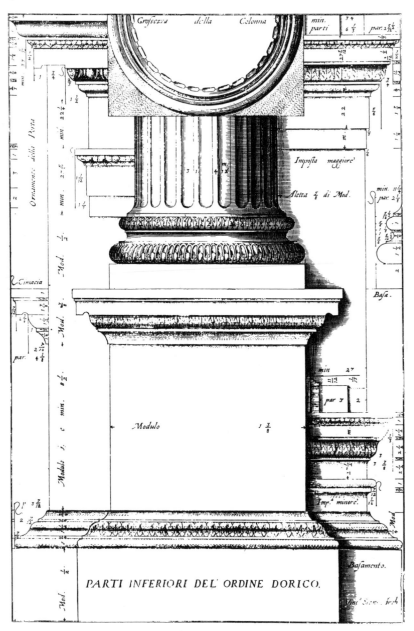

PARTI INFERIORI DEL ORDINE DORICO.

b

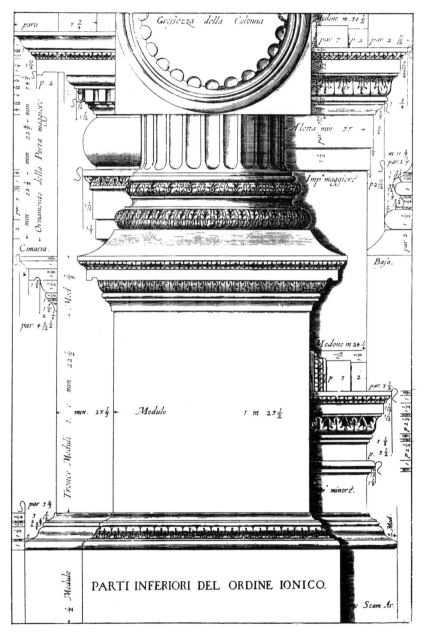

Grossezza della Colonna

Medone m. 30 ½

Altezza min. 35

Imp.ª maggiore

Cimacia.

Baja.

Modone m. 24 ¼

Modulo   1 m 23½

minor è.

PARTI INFERIORI DEL ORDINE IONICO.

Scam Ar.

c

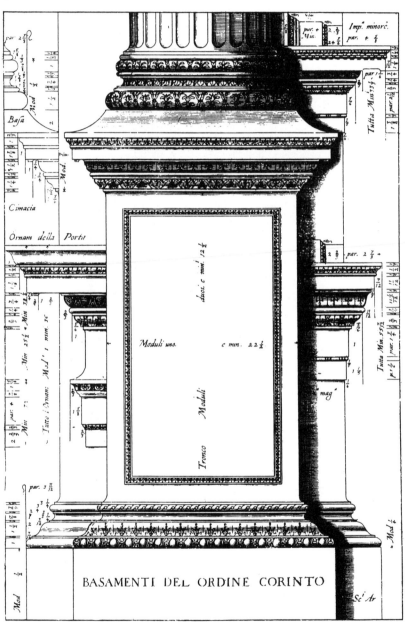

BASAMENTI DEL ORDINE CORINTO

d

BASAMENTI DEL ORDINE ROMANO.

22. Doric entablature with an acroterion in the form of acanthus leaves and with a raking sima supporting a drain pipe concealed in a lion's head.

23. Fragments of antefixes (Fiechter and Thiersch 1906).

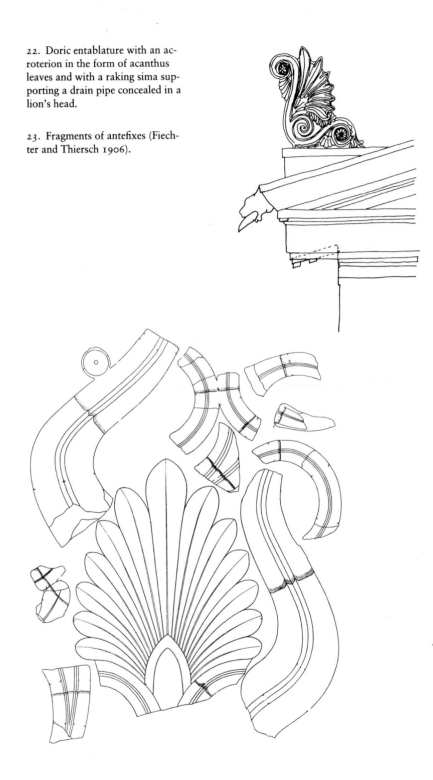

on the architrave below; and (3) the *architrave,* also made up of blocks, which span the distance between two columns and rest on the capitals. Architraves form a beamlike continuous band, flush with the extremities of the capitals. This division holds for all the genera.

The column (see figure 19b), in turn, breaks down into (1) the *capital,* the topmost member; (2) the *shaft,* the middle portion; and (3) the *base,* the lower part. Only in the Doric genus, where the base is frequently absent, does there seem to be an exception to the rule of tripartition.

The stylobate or crepidoma, the platform from which the column rises, also keeps to the tripartite division by virtue of the three steps it normally has.

When there is a pedestal (see figures 20, 21, 89) between the column and stylobate, it too is divided into (1) the *cornice,* projecting in the form of a continuous eave; (2) the *dado,* a block of varying height; and (3) the *pedestal base.*

As we move to more detailed subdivisions, the differences between genera are increasingly accentuated. The cornice (see figures 20, 22, 24c, 24d, 29), the crowning member of the entablature, is divided into three parts, in descending sequence:

1. The row of *antefixes,* upright individual members adorned with flabelliform patterns, usually anthemions, palmettes, or lotuses (see figure 23). Above the three angles of the pediment, the antefixes are replaced by the *acroteria,* decorative members, usually in the form of griffons, sphinxes, chimeras, or oversized acanthus leaves (see figure 22). These tend to be left out of Renaissance engravings in spite of their importance in antique classical buildings.

2. The *sima* (not to be confused with the cyma, a molding), a continuous gutter, in early times of terra cotta, then of marble, pierced with spouts generally concealed in carved lions' heads (see figures 22, 29) and ending in a curve.

3. The *geison* or *corona,* continuous stone eaves projecting beyond the frieze below and ending in a straight vertical line. The geison is sometimes doubled. The *coffer,* or underside, of the Doric geison is traditionally adorned with *mutules* (see figure 46e), sloping flat blocks carrying eighteen *guttae* and separated by spaces called *viae* (see figure 29, 46c, 46d). In the other genera, the ornament varies greatly.

This is the tripartite division of the cornice as seen laterally. Observed from the facade or the back, however, the cornice is gabled; it is slanted upward in order to follow the slope of the triangular pediment, or gable-end, created by the pitched roof above it (see figure 22). Here the

a

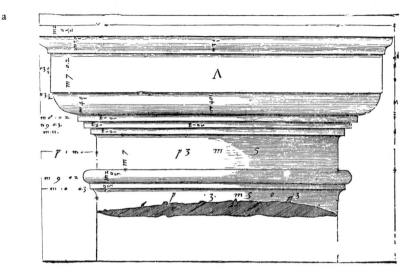

24. (a) Doric capital. (b) Ionic
base. (c, d) Entablatures. All from
Delorme (1576).

b

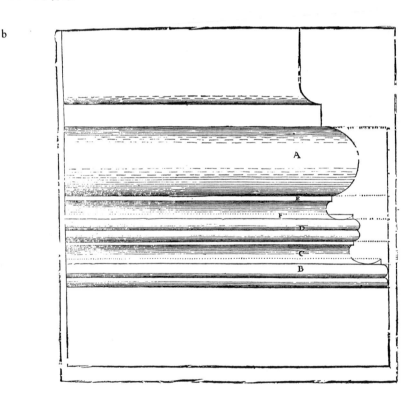

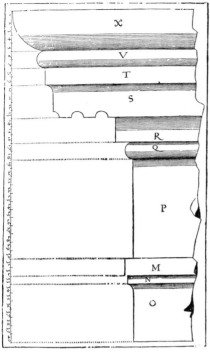

c

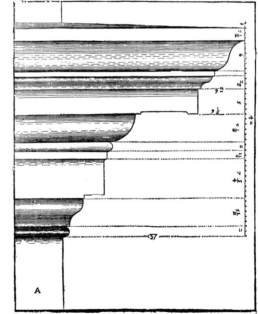

d

lowest member, the geison, remains horizontal, whereas the middle member, the sima, follows the slopes of the roof. These sloping, or *raking*, simas, as they are called, retain an underlying geisonlike band that echoes and replicates the horizontal geison. The disposition of the upper members of the raking cornice, the antefixes and the acroteria, retains the same tripartite organization as in the horizontal.

In the Doric genus, the *frieze* (see figures 25a, 26), the second subdivision of the cornice, is composed horizontally of two alternating motifs. One is the *triglyph*, usually made up of three vertical shanks separated by two deep grooves, or chamfers, with a beveled outer edge on both end shanks. The other motif is the *metope*, a block often bearing carved relief. The triglyphs are upright and rectangular in shape, whereas the metopes are approximately square. The Ionic frieze (see figure 25b) is a continuous band with carved reliefs throughout its full length; hence the name *zoophoros* given to it in Greek, meaning that which carries representations of live things. A canonical example of the *zoophoros* is to be found in the north portico of the temple of the Erechtheion of the fifth century B.C. on the Acropolis of Athens. An alternative to the zoophoros is a continuous band of *dentils,* a row of small, narrowly interspersed rectangular teethlike members (the word *dentils* derives from the Latin *dens,* meaning tooth) and reminiscent of the exposed ends of rafters present in the timber construction of the prototypical Ionic temples. This is the case with the Treasuries of Delphi, built in the sixth century B.C., and with the Temple of Athena Polias in Priene, built in the fourth. After this time, the frieze tends to be a *zoophoros* combined with smaller dentils that run along its upper edge. This is the combination adopted by Vitruvius (*De Architectura,* bk. III, ch. V, para. 11). It is also illustrated in Serlio (1619, bk. IV, ch. VI, para. 170; see figure 19) and in Perrault (1673; see figure 25b).

Coming to the third member of the tripartite Doric cornice, the architrave, or *epistylion* (see figure 29), is usually broken down into (1) the *taenia,* a narrow and beamlike strip, slightly cantilevered over the member below; (2) the *regula,* a narrow fillet beneath the taenia, onto which are attached at regular intervals the *guttae,* a row of six pendant cylinders or cones (see figure 46e); and (3) the *architrave* proper.

In the Ionic genus, the architrave (see figure 20) is also divided into three members, called the *fasciae* (see figures 28c, 28d), flat horizontal members, the top two slightly cantilevered beyond that below. In addition, the upper edge of the upper fascia is terminated by the so-called *architrave molding,* which in the most pure canonical cases, such as the fifth-century Nike temple (figure 33) and the Erechtheion on the Acropolis of Athens (figure 27), is divided into (1) a *fillet* combined with a *cavetto* or *trochilus,* an unadorned concave molding; (2) a Lesbian cymation, or cyma reversa (see figures 39, 41d). This is a band molded with a leaf-and-dart pattern. It is curved outward more fully at the top and inward toward the bottom. One might also find an Ionic cymation (see figures 39, 41c), a convex egg-and-dart molding that is quirked, that is, set off by an indentation; and (3) an *astragal,* a decorative, semirounded convex molding containing a so-called bead-and-reel pattern of disks alternating with round or elongated beads.

Coming to the capital of the Doric column (see figures 24a, 25a, 29), it breaks down into (1) the *abacus,* an unadorned square panel; (2) the *echinus,* a molding with a spreading convex section, meaning flared at the top; and (3) the *necking,* differentiated from the column by the absence of fluting and by ornamental carvings, as in the Temple of Ceres in Paestum (early sixth century B.C.). Later, the necking takes the form of a series of vertical rings incised over the flutings, which now rise up to the echinus. This is the case of the Parthenon (mid-fifth century B.C.). In Roman architecture, the sinkage is replaced by a ring of moldings.

The Ionic capital (see figures 27, 30–32) has a more complex configuration, but it retains a tripartite division:

1. The abacus, with a *Lesbian cymation* (see figure 39).

2. The *volutes.* From the front, the volutes are traditionally likened to a scroll with its two ends wound up in spirals and bulging over the sides of the column shaft (see figures 30, 31, 33, 34, 52). The sides of the rolls, called *balusters* or bolsters, are bound up vertically through the center by one or a series of moldings decorated in various ways, often as a schematized laurel branch or in the bead-and-reel pattern.

3. The *echinus,* a molding with an Ionic cymation. A palmette carving is usually applied to the points where the echinus disappears under the foldings of both volutes (see figures 31–34).

At the angles of porticos and temples, Ionic capitals display both fronts in perpendicular rather than parallel fashion. This ensures the continuity of each of the intersecting colonnades. The outer common volute projects diagonally between the adjacent fronts. This is the case with

a

25. (a) Doric column with entablature. (b) Ionic column with entablature.

b

Planche XIX

B
C
B'
A

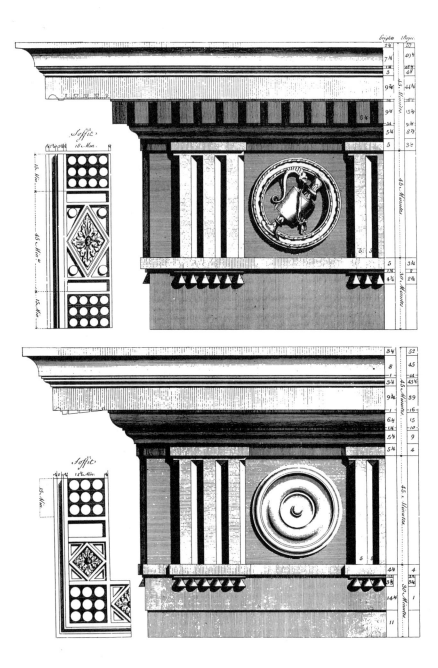

26. Doric entablatures (Chambers 1791).

27. The Erechtheion of Athens, north porch. From Kohte (1915).

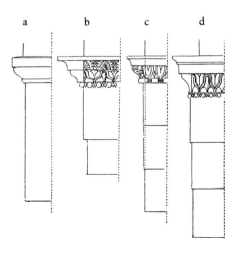

a   b   c   d

28. Ionic architraves. (a) Temple on the Ilissos. (b) Temple of Apollo in Melitos. (c) Temple of Nike, Athens. (d) Erechtheion, Athens.

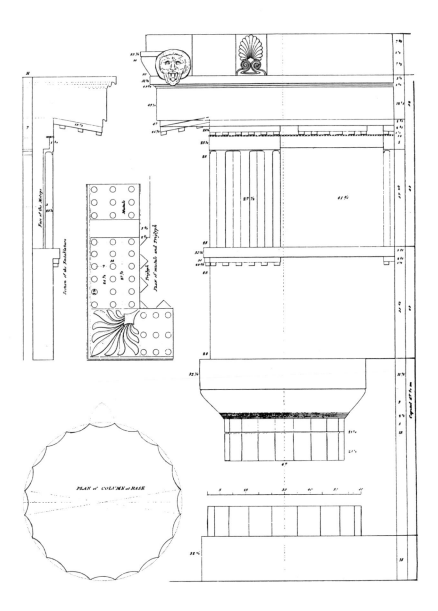

29. Some Doric elements (Lafever
1833).

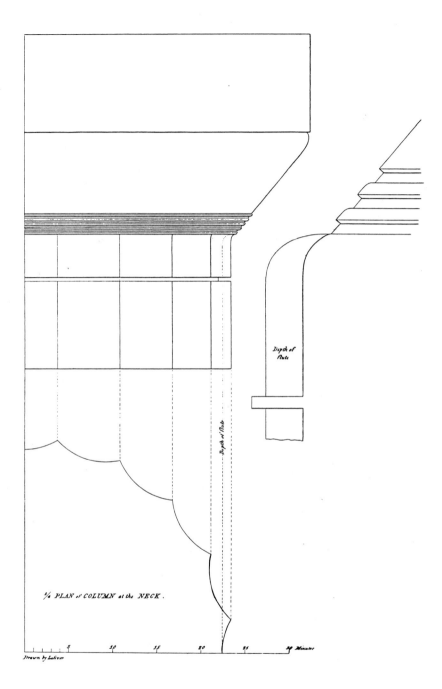

¼ PLAN of COLUMN at the NECK.

Depth of
Flute

Depth of Flute

5   10   15   20   25   30 Minutes

Drawn by Lafever

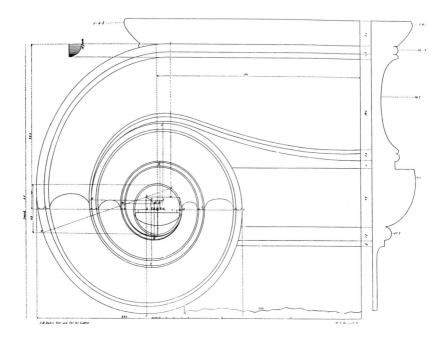

30. Volute from the Ionic temple
on the Ilissos River near Athens
(Lafever 1833).

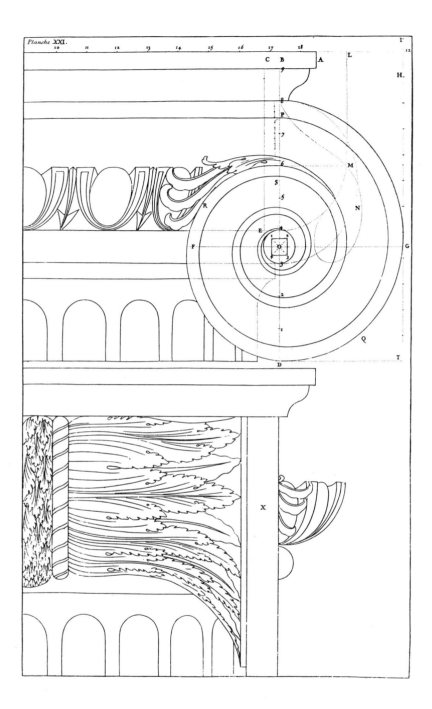

31. Ionic capital (Perrault 1673).

32. Ionic capitals (Delorme 1576).

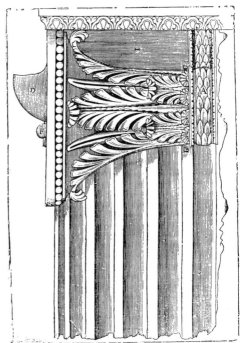

33. Corner capital of the Temple
of Nike (c. 425 B.C.), Athens.
From Kohte (1915).

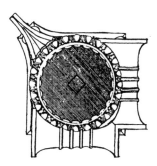

34. Corner capital of the Temple
of Fortuna Virilis, Rome (Palladio
1570).

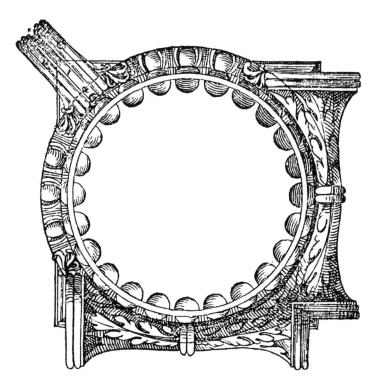

the classical Ionic temples, such as the Temple of Nike at Athens (figure 33). Palladio, to whom the Greek prototypes were unknown—they were unknown, in fact, until the publication of Le Roy's *Ruines des plus beaux monument de la Grèce* (1758) and Stuart and Revett's *Antiquities of Athens* (1762)—wrongly attributes the "beautiful and graceful invention" of placing fronts at a ninety degree angle to the Roman temple of Fortuna Virilis (Palladio 1570, bk. IV, ch. XIII; figure 34).

The shaft of the Doric column remains undivided horizontally, whereas vertically it is divided into twenty usually shallow flutes separated by their sharply wedged edges or *arrises* (see figures 29, 54, 55). The upper and lower extremities of the Ionic shaft are shaped in a concave curve called the *apophyge,* which can be followed by a narrow, flat unornamented band called the fillet and by a bead-and-reel patterned molding (see figures 25b, 28a). The Ionic shaft is divided into twenty-four flutes, usually relatively deep, elliptical in section, and separated by a narrow flat strip.

The base of the column is generally absent in the Doric genus (see figure 25a). When a Doric column does rest on a base, as is frequently the case in the Renaissance—in Serlio (1619), for example (see figure 19), and occasionally in Palladio (1570; see figures 20, 64, 84, 85)—it adopts the articulation of the Ionic base. The Ionic base underwent continuous change before the fifth century B.C. (see figure 59), when it arrived at its most canonical form in the temples of Nike and the Erechtheion (figures 27, 59j) in Athens. The Ionic Ilissos Temple (figure 59h) destroyed in the nineteenth century but fortunately documented by Stuart and Revett in 1762, was also canonical. In these three structures the tripartite organization became prominent, the members being (1) the *torus,* a convex molding; (2) the *scotia, trochilus,* or *cavetto,* a deeply concave molding; and (3) another *torus.* In other Ionic temples the lower torus was replaced by the plinth, as in the Apollo Temple in Miletos (figure 59e) and the Temple of Athena Polias in Priene (figure 59k) or in the Perrault (1673) example (figure 25b). Sometimes, however, one finds a plinth supporting the entire torus-scotia-torus unit, as in the Inner Propylaea of Appius Claudius Pulcher at Eleusis of the first century B.C. (figure 59m), or as in Palladio (1570; figure 64) and Perrault (1673; figures 25b, 35). This is the solution favored by Vitruvius himself (see *De Architectura,* bk. III, ch. V, para. 1ff). It is possible to elaborate further the torus and the scotia through horizontal fluting. In addition, the scotia itself can be multiplied into two scotiae or *trochili,* as in the Apollo Temple in Miletos (figure 59l) and the Temple of Athena Polias in Priene (figure 59k), with the two scotiae inserted between three layers of *double astragals* or *roundels.* In the Temple of Hera (sixth century B.C.) in Samos (figure 59f), the lower part of the base is composed of no less than six fluted scotiae sandwiched between seven double astragals.

So far we have concentrated on examples of the Doric and Ionic genera. This is because they are most typical. One can easily generalize this analysis to apply to the rest of the genera, which never became genera in the same sense as the two older forms. The only distinguishing traits of the Corinthian genus are the *modillion* (see figures 20, 87), a horizontal scrolled bracket or console attached under the geison in the same manner as the Doric mutule (see figure 29), and the particular form of the capital. In every other way, in Vitruvius's own words, the Corinthian is similar to the Ionic (*De Architectura,* bk. IV, ch. I, para. 1).

A number of important sculptor-architects were involved in the development of the Corinthian capital—Scopas at the Temple of Athena Alea at Tegea and the younger Polyclitos at the Tholos of Epidauros and possibly even Iktinos at the Temple of Apollo Epikourios at Bassai (Carpenter 1970, p. 152). The Corinthian capital is tripartite, like that of the other genera. As with the Ionic capital, at the top is the abacus section (see figures 36, 37, 39a, 39b), itself comprising three sections: a small convex cymation, an even more slender taenia, and a somewhat tall cavetto at the bottom. After the abacus comes a volute, followed by one row of acanthus leaves curled outward, superimposed on another. This tripartite section rests on an astragal that marks the necking (see figures 36, 37).

The Other Elements

There is a tendency to regard the genera as applying to the columnar elements only, to consider that the difference between a Doric and an Ionic temple, for example, resides merely in the configuration of capitals, bases, and architraves. In fact, the scope of the genus formal level is far broader. To begin with, it includes the pedestal (see figure 21), which serves as a base for the column and which can also be used as a freestanding support for a statue or as an independent upright block, as in the case of antique altars or memorials. Other architectural elements formed by the genera are the *pillar,* a freestanding support of square or oblong section, and the *pilaster* (or *parastas*), formed by thickening the wall at the end or at certain points and treated as a sliced or an engaged pillar attached to the side or to the end of a wall (see figures 41, 77, 78). Since the Renaissance, the balustrades of balconies or stairs (Wittkower 1974, p. 43) have also been constrained by the formal renditions of the genera. The vertical supports, known as *banisters,* correspond to the column and are articulated as colonnettes, with their own abacus, ovolo, torus, and cavetto, borrowing the Tuscan, Doric, Ionic, or Corinthian capital and base (see figures 73, 84). One might also say that the typical curve of its *bulb* member is an exaggerated entasis of the shaft of the column. The lower rail is seen as the crepidoma. Every vertical corporal unit of whatever size—wall, parapet, platform—that becomes part of a classical building is subject to the same treatment. It is divided, molded, and proportioned according to the canon level of the genera. The openings of the building also are identified by the same formal level of the genera. Doors, windows, and niches are categorized, apart from proportions to which we refer shortly, by their genera markers, such as the cymation ornaments (see figure 38), or by their colonnettes, *pediment,* or *fronton,* a triangular or curved element similar to the end of a roof of a classical building (see figure 44). The *antepagment,* a facing that frames the opening head and jambs by moldings appropriately shaped and proportioned, is another important indicator of genus (see figures 43, 45). Finally, ceilings, floor pavements, and door panelings (see figures 44, 46, 47) can be made out of units that adhere to the discipline of the genera by having the proportions and moldings of their constituent panels coffered and engaged in rendered cases.

REFINEMENTS

So far we have given, necessarily, a condensed description of the subdivisions of the genera. We have had to omit many exceptions to the canon. We have not, for example, touched on the constant evolution of the configuration of the Doric members, their proportions, and their divisions. The echinus of the Doric capital is perhaps most illustrative of this evolution. Its early form is more flared at top, as in the sixth-century Temple of Ceres in Paestum. After the fifth century the echinus

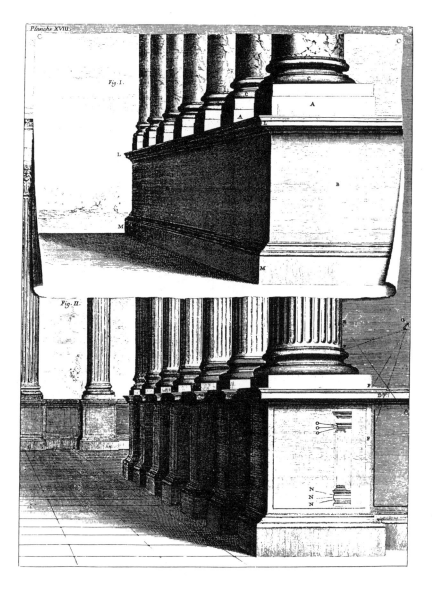

36. Corinthian capitals (Delorme
1576).

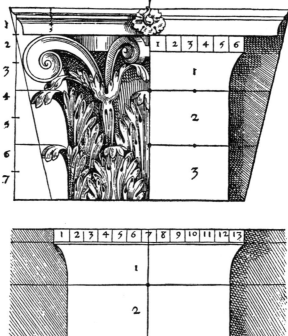

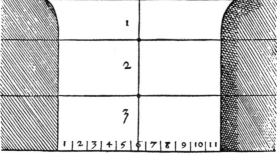

Corniche des
frontons pointus.

Corniche des
frontons ronds.

Chapiteau des Colonnes dessiné sur l'Angle.

Plan du Chapiteau des Colonnes renversé.

ffitte de l'Architraue

Profil de l'Architra.

1 module   28 parties

37. Corinthian capital, architrave,
and cornice from the Pantheon in
Rome (Desgodetz 1682).

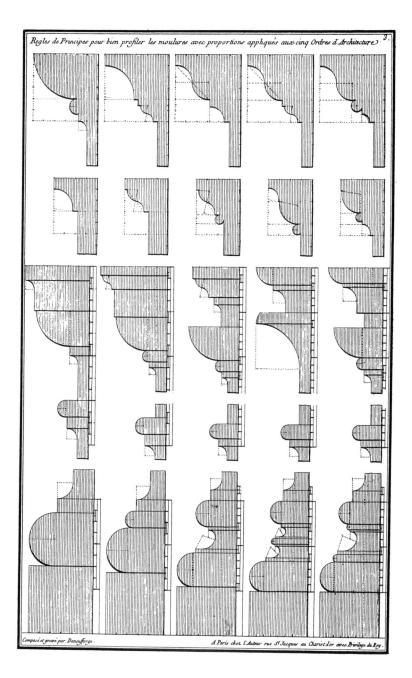

38. The molding profiles with
their proper proportions, as applied to the five genera (Neufforge
1757–1780).

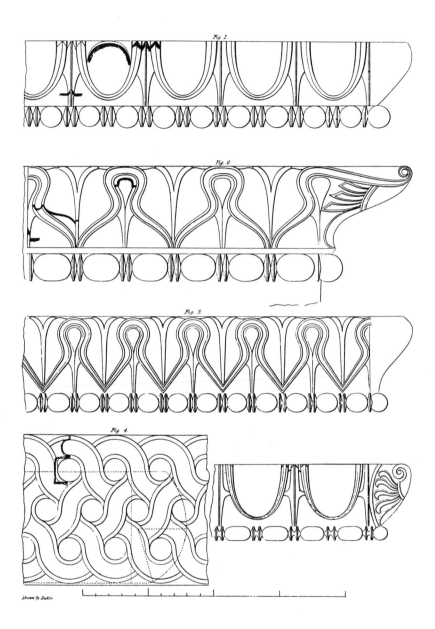

39. Ionic and Lesbian cymatia
(Lafever 1833).

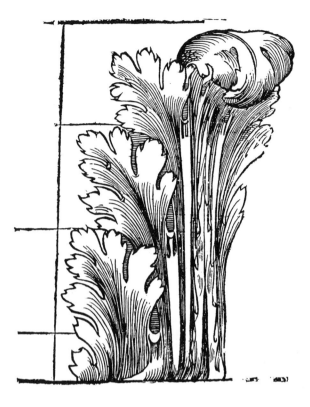

40. Ornaments (Delorme 1576).

a 𝔓arf𝔥mon.   Selinus

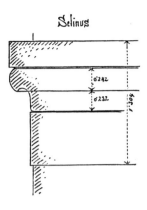

41. (a) The Doric cymation on the
cornice of the Parthenon and of
the Temple "C" of Selinus. (b)
Ionic pilaster from the Erechtheion
with rows of Lesbian and Ionic
cymations. (c) Ionic cymation
from the Erechtheion. (d) Lesbian
cymation from the Erechtheion.
All from Durm (1915).

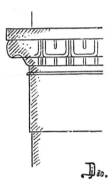

b

c

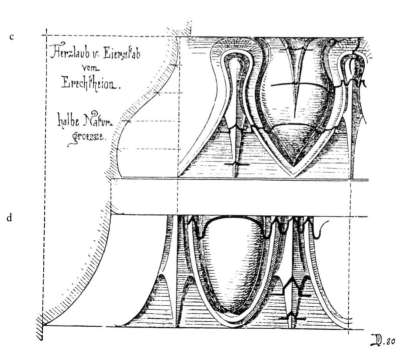

Herzlaub v. Eierstab
vom
Erechtheion.

halbe Natur-
groesse.

d

D.80

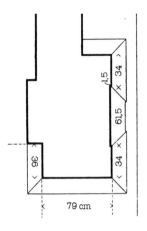

42. Section of an Ionic pilaster from the Erechtheion, Athens. Kohte (1915).

43. Ionic door frame from the Erechtheion.

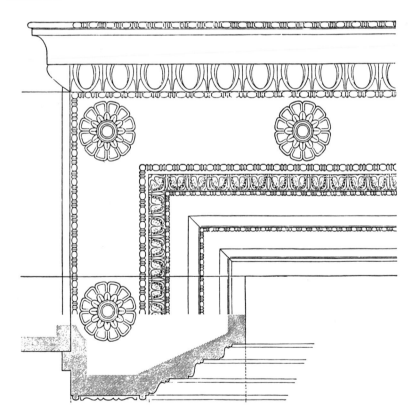

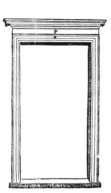

44. Genera as applied to window frames and to doors (Serlio 1619).

45. A Corinthian window frame
(Scamozzi 1615).

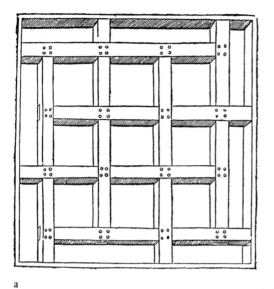

a

46. (a) Grid and tripartition applied to ceiling (Serlio 1619). (b) Ionic coffering on a ceiling (Serlio 1619). (c) The Corinthian coffer of the Temple of Mars the Avenger in Rome (Palladio 1570). (d) The Corinthian coffer of the tetrastyle hall of a portico (Palladio 1570). (e) Underside, or soffit, of a Doric geison (Perrault 1673).

b

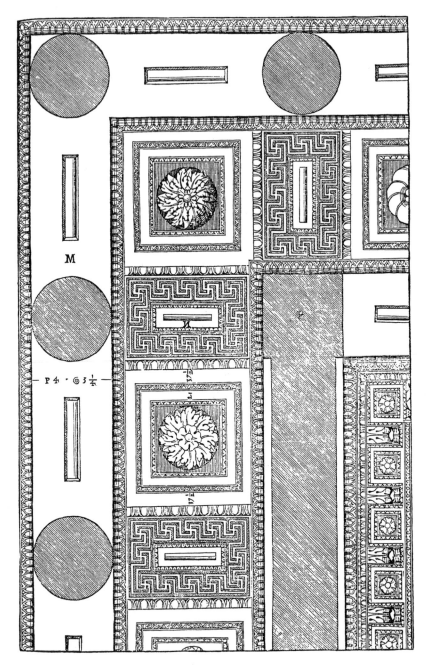

M

P 4 · ⊙ 3¼

c

46 continued

d

e

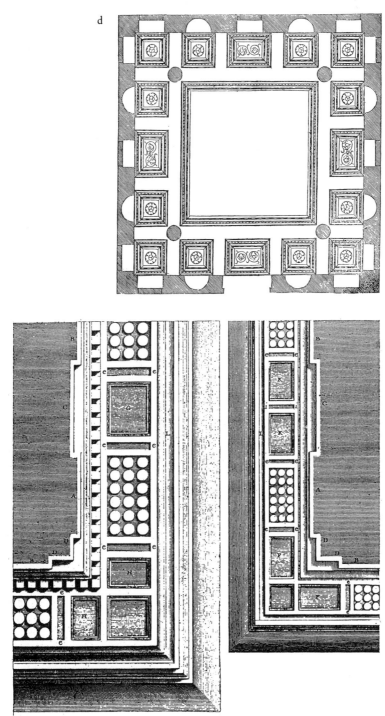

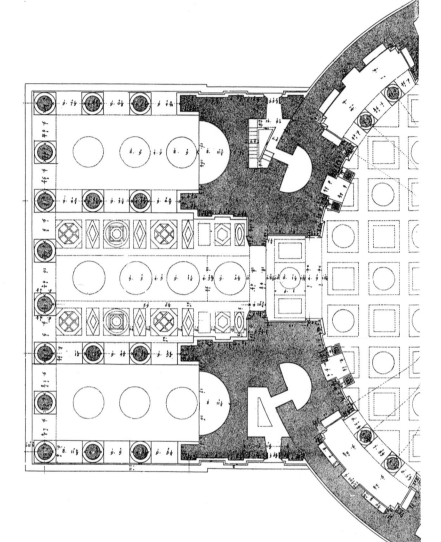

47. The floor pavement of the
Pantheon of Rome (Desgodetz
1682).

became more compact, its curve attenuated until it almost resembled a truncated cone. Similar transformations characterize the shape of the Doric shaft as it becomes more slender, with a less pronounced entasis, or bulge toward the middle, between the sixth and the second century B.C. We have not described alterations even more complex in other members, not only of the Doric genus but of the other genera as well. Neither have we discussed the special cases of columns that appeared in antiquity, which, for reasons unknown to us, display members at variance from those enumerated here. Such exceptions are the hybrid, mysterious bull-Doric capital of the column-pier of Python Hall at Hellenistic Delos or the even more intriguing fusion of Doric capital with Ionic consoles from the Throne of Apollo at Amyclae (second half of the sixth century), which, as Robertson (1971, p. 105) writes, tempts us "to speculate how Greek architecture" (and as a matter of fact, classical architecture) "might have developed, had the Doric and Ionic traditions effected a real and fruitful fusion at the beginning of the fifth century." Nor have we referred to the cases of the half-curved shafts with figures in high relief of the Artemision of Ephesos or the half-fluted ones of the lower Doric colonnade of the Stoa of Attalos in Hellenistic Athens. Nor, again, have we examined the bell-shaped palm capitals to be found in Delphi in the Massalian Treasury of the sixth century B.C. or in Hellenistic times at the library of Pergamon and the Stoa of Attalos in Athens. This is because the aim, as stated already, is to indicate common aspects of classical architecture, the overall formal canon, which appears throughout its development.

We have had to ignore the problem of optical illusions and the formal "subtleties" associated with the Doric genus. In fact, we have left aside the attributes that can be described as deviations from the *assumed* regularity: such as in the Doric corner columns which are enlarged and tilted. The earliest evidence of this is to be found in the Sanctuary of Aphaia at Aegina of the late sixth century B.C., and it is a practice generally recommended by Vitruvius (*De Architectura*, bk. III, ch. III, para. iii). The Doric shaft has a slight convexity, the entasis in its taper, and its stylobate is curved. Vitruvius also recommended the tilting of "all the features above the capitals of the columns" toward their fronts by one-twelfth their total height (*De Architectura*, bk. II, ch. V, para. 13) in the Ionic temple. He varied the number of the flutes of the shaft depending on the position of the column (*De Architectura*, bk. IV, ch.

IV, para. 2). All these are practices, justified, as "refinements" (Good-year 1912). They should not be mixed with what the late Renaissance theoreticians of architecture called "abuses." Nor were they manner-isms, although mannerism was connected with discussions on refine-ments. Refinements were not intended as deviations from the canon. Far from it. Their role was to reinforce the canon by compensating for "optical distortions." In other words they corrected *apparent* distor-tions and restored the work to its proper order perceptually.

The problem of refinements has occupied a major place in the litera-ture of classical architecture from the time of Vitruvius. (*De Architec-tura,* bk. III, ch. V; bk. IV, ch. III, IV). One of the most interesting later accounts is given by Claude Perrault (1673) in his commentary on the Vitruvian passages on this issue. Yet despite the importance of this problem, we do not see it as part of our study because formal subtleties relate to perceptual rather than conceptual issues of classical architec-ture, to how the formal patterns of classical architecure are sensed and how they have to be pragmatically constructed, as opposed to how these patterns have been formally conceived within the system of the logos opticos.

All these appendixes to the canon do not violate the rule system of tripartition of classical architecture. First, from the formal point of view, they are not real formal anomalies. Second, their impact on classi-cal achitecture as it has emerged since the Renaissance has not been crucial.

PROPORTIONS

But now let us move to the relation between individual genera and proportions. All members of the genera and all their subdivisions are subject to them. They constrain the relative sizes through the applica-tion of a universal unit system, based on half the diameter of the col-umn, the *module,* or *embates* in Greek. This applies to columns as well as to the rest of the elements of the building. Pilasters, walls, pedestals, balustrades, doors, windows, ceilings, floors, even rooms, are seen as elementary units subject to the constraints of the genera. Let us look at the canon of proportion in more detail as it applies to columns, only though for the sake of clarity.

According to Vitruvius, the module establishes "correspondence" between each "of the separate members even the smallest details to the whole body" of the genus (*De Architectura*, bk. III, ch. I; see figures 49, 50). In the Doric case, for example, he recommends fourteen modules for the entire height of the column (see figure 20), one module for the height of the capital, and two and one-sixth modules for its width. The height of the architrave, including its taenia and its guttae, is one module, and the taenia is one-seventh of the module in height (see figure 48). For the triglyph Vitruvius recommends a height of one and a half modules and a width of one module. The metopes are square in proportion. The half-metopes at the end corners are half a module in width, and the triglyph capitals one-sixth of a module. The cornice above the triglyph capitals projects two-thirds of a module. The total height of the corona is half a module. The list is longer and even more detailed, the proportion grid specifying every minute wave of matter down to the smallest particle, the most slender cymation or taenia, of the artifact (see figures 51, 53).

The proportions of the members of the Ionic columnar element are set up by Vitruvius in a similar manner in relation to the thickness of the column, always referring to its lowest part. The total height of the column varies from eight to ten times its diameter, depending on the distance between columns. This intricate correspondence is discussed in more detail in the next chapter on symmetry, where the rules of intercolumniation are analyzed. For the total base of the column Vitruvius suggests half of the thickness of the column. The same proportion is mentioned for the height of the capital, including the volutes, thus underlining the affinity between the two end members of the columnar element. The architraves (see figure 48) vary from half the thickness of the column to one-twelfth the height of the column, depending on the height of the column. The cymation of the architrave is one-seventh of the architrave's total height. The rest of the architrave is sectioned into twelve units, three of which are for the lowest of the fasciae and four and five for the subsequent ones, for reasons more optical than conceptual. The frieze is one-fourth less or more than the height of the architrave, depending on whether or not it carries reliefs. The dentils and the geisons are the same height as the middle fascia. Finally, the height of the sima is one-eighth more than that of the geison. As in the case of the Doric genus, the relative height and width of all members of the Ionic are specified through the device of the module, spreading an invisible grid schema over each of the genera (see figure 48).

Between the recommendations of Vitruvius and the proportions to be found in the classical buildings of antiquity there are some differences in the details but not in the logic. Vitruvius's list of interrelated dimensions indeed give us an accurate idea of the proportioning of the genera throughout the whole classical tradition.

MODULATIONS

Through the genera, architectural elements as varied as columns and pedestals, arches and walls, windows and doors, niches and chimneys, are rendered into correlative members, subdivided and proportioned in homologous ways and made to embody similar shapes. By aquiring certain common attributes, elements that differ in volume, function, or location are recognized as belonging to one family, to one genus as distinct from another. Conversely, elements similar in volume or function can be differentiated.

A door for example is bordered by a frame, a *chambranle,* which displays the ornaments that act as genus "markers" if you will. As one can clearly see in the north door of Erechtheion, the lintel and the sides of the door incorporate in a microcosmic way the entablature of the Ionic temple (see figures 41, 43).

Genera are exceptionally assigned to a single element of a building. They are usually applied to the whole or at least to a part of a building. In this whole or part, all elements have a deep formal kinship, a coherence in the organization of their features, a consistency in the manner in which these features are structured. This division of the building into zones, we might say, within which all elements have a subtle affinity, brings to mind the way classical music works are organized.

In classical music there can be a change in key, a change in tonality, when one moves from one part of a piece to another or even from one part of a part of the composition to another. So in classical architecture there can be a shift in genus, in the modality of the elements. There can be a change from the Doric to the Ionic, or from the Ionic to the Corinthian, while the building unfolds within the structure of taxis from one part to another or from one part of a part to another. Such

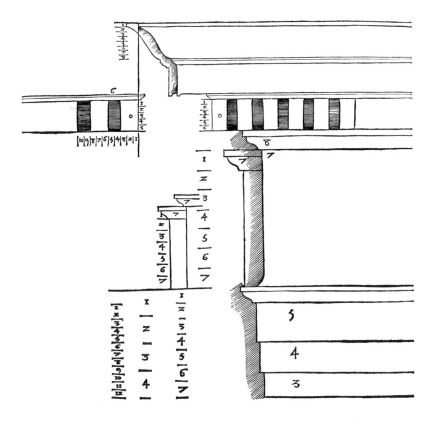

48. Proportions as applied to an
Ionic entablature (Martin 1547).

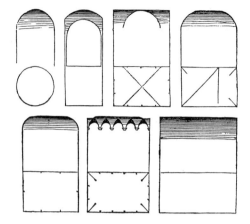

49. Proportions applied to the interior of a room. (a) Palladio (1570). (b) Scamozzi (1615). (c) Cesariano (1521). (d) Cesariano (1521).

a

b

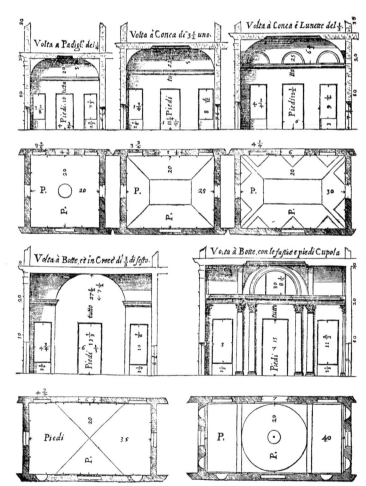

c

d

IONICARVM SPIRARVM EX DIVERSIS MEMBRIS SYM/
METRIATIS PERMVTATISQ₂ TORIS AC SVPERCILIS FIGVRA⋅

SPIRAE SEV BASIS PERSERVIĒTIS VARIIS COLVMNARVM GENE/
RIBVS QVADRATIS   VEL ATIGVRGIS
PEREIGVRATIO⋅

SVB SPIRA STYLOBATI TRVNCVS SEV ARVLA
INTERCOLVMNARIS PERAEQVATVR⋅

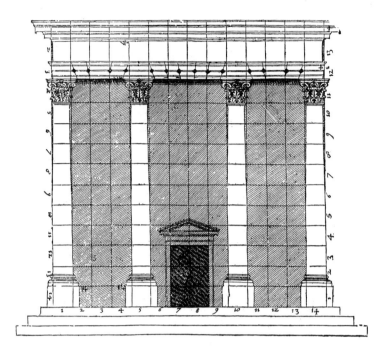

50. Proportions applied to facades
(Delorme 1576).

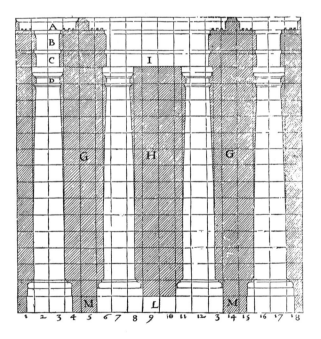

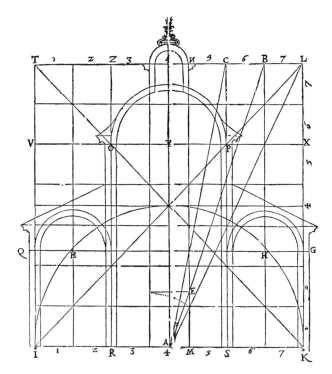

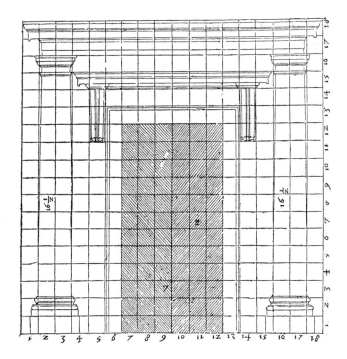

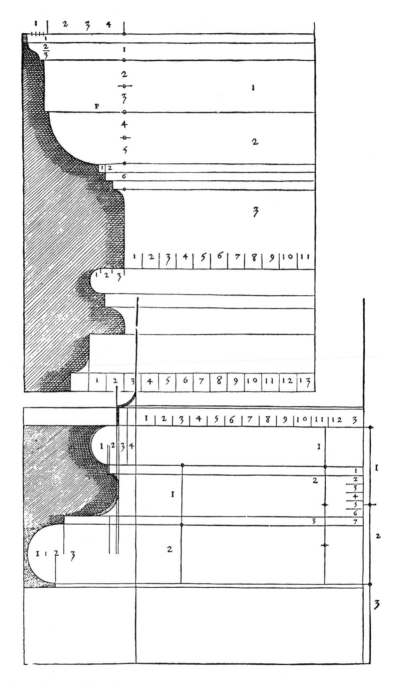

51. Proportions applied to (a) a
Doric capital and (b) Ionic
bases (Martin 1547).

b

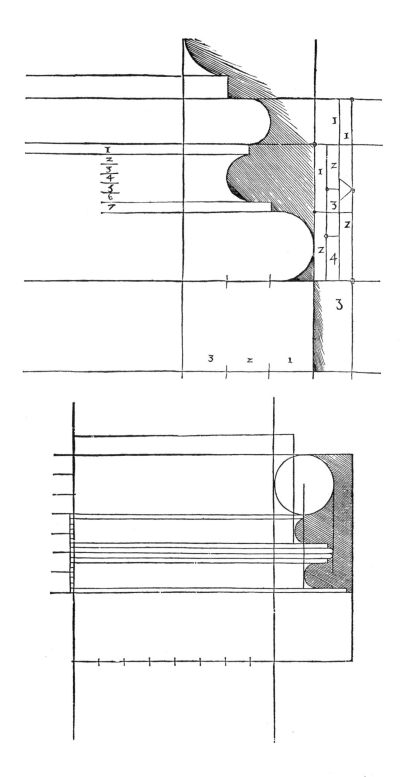

changes in key, which we call *modulations* in classical music, are not only permissible but also essential. Similarly, in classical architecture, shifts in genus, which we can also call *modulations,* are important. We discuss the mechanisms of architectural modulation in the next chapter.

NESTED HIERARCHIES

Let us look at the overall organization of the subdivisions of a classical building once more. Because our main concern here is with the genera themselves, we look at how these are internally ordered and how their hierarchically nested components, which we have just enumerated, are formally composed through the tripartite schema. We examine how the elements are partitioned step by step into member-parts and these into ornaments and, conversely, how ornaments are grouped progressively into member-parts and these into elements. Of concern, too, is how space is divided, how its divisions are discerned, how space is assembled, and how its units are joined.

We have already accepted three steps of nested subdivisions: ornaments within member-parts, member-parts within members, and members within the genus elements—almost all put together according to the schema of tripartition. Because, on the other hand, in practice even small ornaments can be found broken down into finer details, as "microcymatia" or "microtaeniae," we have to admit the existence of one more step of analysis of embedded units within the elements (see figures 39, 41, 53). We have, therefore, four steps of subdivision. Yet, the troubles of formal componential dissection are not over. Details and microdetails can be taken further apart to identify the geometrical determinants that give them their shape. Take the Lesbian cymation. How concave or convex is its outline? The precise definition of its curves depends on the axes, foci, and asymptotes—if we consider them to be hyperbolic as the Greeks probably did (Coulton 1977, p. 107)—or on the radii and the position of the centers of their circles—if we take them to be made out of parts of circles, as Renaissance architects did and many architects since have (see figures 49a, 53).

Ever since antiquity there has been an unresolved debate about the degree of precision with which architectural details ought to be controlled, the need to specify down to this fifth and perhaps sixth step, the

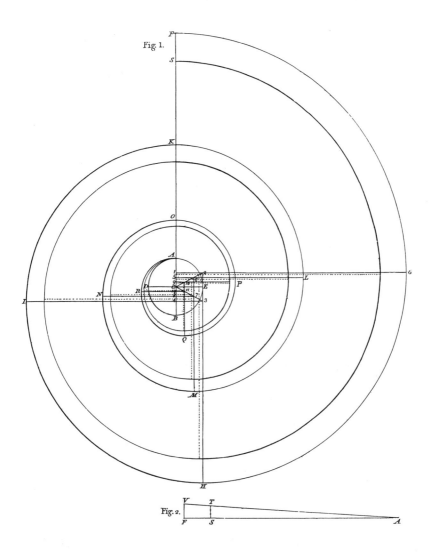

52. Geometric constructions of Ionic volutes (Chambers 1791).

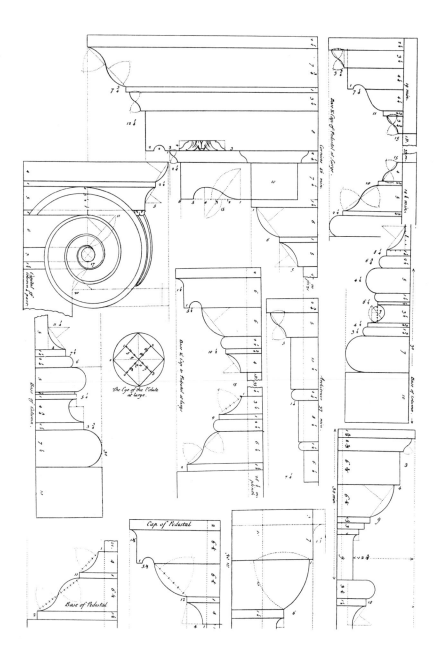

53. Geometric constructions constraining molding profiles (Pain
1762).

extent of exactitude premeditated, to which the fifth-century sculptor Polykleitos referred to as *para micron* (Coulton 1977, p. 109).

Such a preoccupation with bits of matter and geometry might be seen as an academic exercise into formal trivia. Much of the uniqueness of classical contours, of the specifics of the physiognomy of the classical genera, on the other hand, depends on the rigor with which formal structure is conceived in terms of formal atoms on the hierarchies within which these atoms are interlocked. It springs out of the clarity and transparency of these formal conceptions; the devising of small, simple plans of composition and then their consistent assembly into total organizations; and the commitment to a level of control over form, and once this is defined, to the obsession with tilting, tapering, and curling of minute details while ensuring the coherence of the whole.

CONTOUR PATTERNS

Now that the components and steps of subdivision of the genera have been identified, we can turn to the logic through which these components are put together. We proceed from the elementary level of the genera down to their details.

There are several ways of structuring space, but within the formal system of classical architecture two paths have traditionally been open: *metric patterns* and *contour motion*. The case is once more similar to music and poetry. In music, patterns are generated both by rhythm, the regular alternation of accentuated and nonaccentuated sounds, and by modifications of pitch, the location of the musical sound in the tonal scale. In poetry, patterns are born also out of rhythm, arrangements alternating periodically stressed and unstressed syllables, as well as the contiguity and combinations of speech sounds, so-called phonemes, which create rhyming, alliteration, contrast, and variation.

In architecture, classical contour patterns arise from the regulated stream of surges, swirls, and whirlpools of solid matter. These small fractions of sequence—the curved ones are referred to as "little waves" or *cymatia* (see figures 38, 39)—make up, more than an assortment, almost a dictionary of appearances. Let us imagine this dictionary listed in the form of two columns of opposed entries. This form of data organization, corresponding to what Jakobson et al. (1952) called "binary oppositions," provides a clear and easy way of looking at and choosing from among contour shape characteristics. Here is the list:

protruding   indented

straight   curved

convex   concave

flat   inclined

When we create a classical architectural profile, we pick out certain characteristics from this list and conjoin them. We can maintain the identity of a shape through *repetition* or by partially changing it through *reduction* or *amplification*. Finally, we can alter it by *inversion* or by *inflection*.

These means might seem scarce and simple, but the possibilities that arise from their combination, one might almost say conjugation, are enormous. It is these combinations that classical architects have employed and exploited within the tightest constraints. The most memorable invention of classical architecture—the Doric shaft—is perhaps the most obvious illustration of binary oppositions.

The most striking relation between coutour shapes in the horizontal section of the Doric shaft is repetition, an almost obsessive pattern (see figures 36a, 54, 55). The concave flutes come together in razor sharp edges, pursuing each other in an endless dance around the circle of the column. Also evident is the relation of inversion, between the convexity of the round shaft and the concavity of the channels that are embedded in it. In addition, there is an inflection setting the curved shaft against the straight stylobate or against the rigid plane of the rigorously aligned columns of a *pteron,* or a front. In circular buildings, as in the fourth-century Tholos in Delphi, one can also speak of reduction between the circular outline of the temple and the circular section of the shaft.

Let us now look at a complete profile of a Tuscan column as drawn in the 1547 French edition of Vitruvius's *De Architectura,* edited by Jean Martin, one of the most important French humanists (see figure 56). Based more or less on the Vitruvian description, this Tuscan column was drawn by Jean Goujon, sculptor, illustrator, and great propagandist of classical architecture in France during the time of François I. Here, relations between contour shape units are not as tightly concentrated as in the pattern of the Doric shaft. Here patterns result from the

54. Section of the Doric column
displaying outline of fluting
(Pikionis 1935).

55. Section of the Doric column
(Martin 1547).

56. Profiles (Serlio 1619).

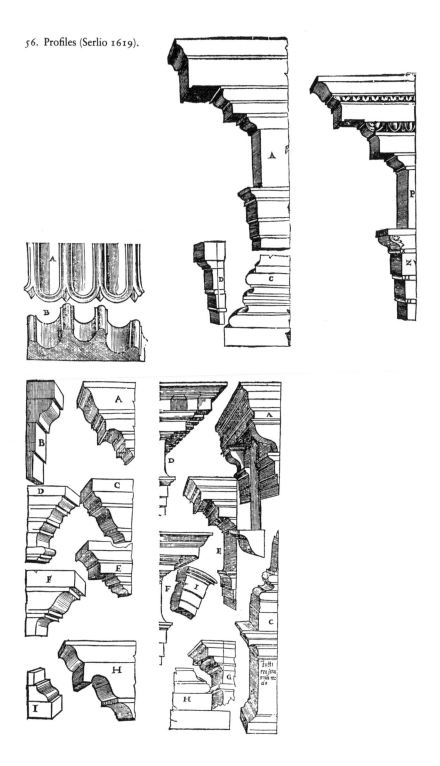

stringing along of shape units rather than from nesting. But there is more than one thing to look at. We see evolving the complete profile of an integral member of the genera. Significantly different in this example of the profile of the Tuscan column is the presence of divisions, beginnings, terminations, and tripartition. In addition, the convex torus of the column base rises above the straight plinth of the stylobate; there is inflection. Inflection also occurs in the beginning of the capital, where the convex small molding known as the astragal succeeds the straight upper fillet of the shaft, only to be succeeded in turn by the straight necking of the capital.

It is possible to see certain contour patterns in these successions and collocations of the Tuscan capital of Jean Martin. First, there is an overriding sequence of inflections governing the whole profile. Without exception a curved unit follows a straight one. Second, there is a series of inversions. With one exception out of five, the convex curve precedes a concave.

Taxis patterns and shape patterns work in a complementary way, forming the profile of a column. Although taxis patterns order space by dividing it into sections of three, of nine, and so forth, independently of direction, shape patterns, which inhabit these divisions, give it directionality. They turn the static sections into the consecutive units of a series; they make them into a series of events in space.

Shape units of a profile do not succeed one another from top to bottom as they do from bottom to top. This contrasts with the characteristic reversibility of the shapes that make up the column when we look at it from right to left and vice versa. In the right-left case we find that shapes correspond to each other perfectly; they obey what is called *bilateral symmetry.* In the horizontal sense, the left side of the column is indiscernible from the right. In the vertical sense, the top differs from the base, but, as we have seen, they are not unrelated. The key sections of the capital result from the systematic inversion of the equivalent sections of the base (see figure 57). They are attached to each other according to another kind of relation, which we can call *progression.* These relations of inversion imply that the concatenation of shapes that make up the vertical profile of the column follow a sequence that is not reversible.

For example, there is a nonreversible relation of inversion between the profiles of capital and base. As each section of the base is recessed

57. Doric profiles (Martin 1547).

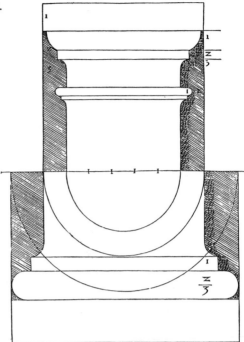

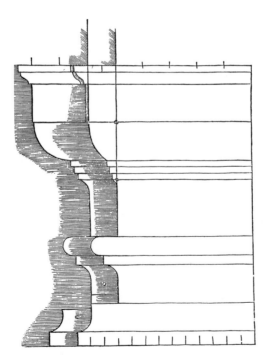

farther inward with height, the topologically equivalent sections of the capital progressively project outward. Renaissance architects carefully stressed the resulting characteristic slope by drawing a *regulatory line* along the outmost members (see figure 36).

From the profile of the columnar member we can proceed to the overall profile of the column, bringing in pediment and stylobate or pedestal. Here we find the same ascents and descents, flutter and glide, immobility and abrupt drops of the moldings—figurative events that, through identity and contrast, similarity and inversion, deflection and amplification, punctuate breaks and extensions, produce the same kind of schemata progression of the profiles of the five genera (see figure 56).

Let us look at the canonical three genera of classical architecture as a series for a moment (see figure 20). At one end, the Doric is divided into a few brief, plain members. At the other end, the Composite has so many members that they almost seem to gesticulate and intertwine. Obviously we have an increasing complexity here, an augmentation of subsections. What the Doric does with one single contour unit—for example, the one torus base—the Composite can take up to six or seven units to do through embedding and amplification. This applies to other members besides the base. The single Doric abacus, for example, is subdivided into three sections in the Ionic and into five in the Corinthian. The architrave, a single unit in the Doric, is sectioned into five units in the Ionic and into seven in the Corinthian. At each genus step more details are added to the same section; more shape events are compressed within the same stretch of space.

This brings us full circle to the point made at the beginning of this chapter. We can now elaborate further: The genera form a level of formal constraints that organize an architectural composition and complement the taxis. Although taxis governs the relation of part to whole, the genera dictate the direction, seriation, and hierarchy of the parts. Through the configuration of their profile, the genera make us understand and control space in a particular way. They have the built-in capacity to do so because they are internally organized as a string of shape contour patterns that can represent progressions and because they can be structured in terms of discrete steps and hierarchies.

It should be clear by now that the moldings—the cymatia, the bead, the fillet, the scotia, and the cavetto—or so-called ornaments of the classical genera, are not in the least "ornamental" and "decorative" in the sense of a frivolous adjunct of an almost superfluous elaboration. They are part of the essential structure of the classical system, vital to its poetics of order. Although the moldings affect small-scale aspects of the composition, their impact is major. They can blur distinctions and clarify them. They make terminations invisible, and they can sharply demarcate them. The ornament in classical architecture should not be confused with the ornament in classical music, synonymous with *agréments* or *plaisanteries* and mere improvisation. Neither should it be mistaken for the embellishing frills that designers increasingly applied during the nineteenth century for purposes of conspicuous consumption. The ornaments, in the sense referred to here, can make or break the coherence of a classical composition.

CANON AND EXCEPTIONS

Centuries of classical tradition confirm the canonical profile of the genera. But they also present a large number of exceptions. There was an endless series of experiments on the composition of the Ionic base before and after the renowned Attic tripartite solution of the Erechtheion. How do such alternatives relate to the classical canon?

Indeed the Ionic base has a long and complicated history (see figures 58, 59). The origins of the shape pattern are obscure and certainly linked with pre-aesthetic ideas of divination. The variants during this period of formation do exhibit key aspects of classical composition. The shaft of the third Temple of Hera of Samos (560 B.C.; figure 59b) for example, rises out of a convex section, the torus; an elementary "binary" opposition between torus and shaft has been a constant through centuries of use. There are two sections articulated, juxtaposed, in a basic manner—another elementary "duality" that will remain with the classical canon, a contrast between torus and a supporting disk (a plain or slightly concave cylindrical section with an embedded fluting pattern, made out of six concave roundels, a *spira*).

Tripartition is manifested only gradually. In the Temple of Artemis at Ephesos (sixth century; figure 59d), we find tripartition still implicit in what is referred to frequently as the Asian type of Ionic base. The base includes a torus—with a nested spira pattern—and a complex of shapes, two trochili between double roundels followed by a plinth. If we accept the plinth as an integral part of the column proper, then we must interpret it as a section in itself, the first section of the base. The second middle section is composed of the roundel-trochili combination. The third is the torus. This kind of interpretation is more difficult to apply to Renaissance profiles of the Asiatic version than to these of the archaic Temple of Artemis at Ephesos or of the incredibly elegant Temple of Athena Polias at Priene of c. 340 (figure 59k). In the Ionic bases of these two temples, as the diagram indicates, there is a tacit concave outline that brings together trochili and rings as an embedded pattern within a mildly concave, one might say dormant, scotia. This is not the case in the post-Renaissance versions of the Asiatic base (see figures 49a, 51).

It might be misleading historically, very "Hegelian," but one is tempted to say that all these alternative profiles of the Ionic base were part of a big search, the result of which was the discovery of the Attic base of Erechtheion at Athens around 420 B.C. (figures 27, 59j). The base, whose shape we have already discussed, was developed along with other architectural details with the greatest care. Like the other moldings it was perfectly executed, a feat of detailing that cost even more, according to the records, than the sculpture of the temple! The shape pattern of the base is elementary. Still it contains explicitly almost all key relations out of which a classical profile has been generated—similarity, inversion, inflection—a true microcosm of the whole system of shape patterning worth any efforts that might have led up to it.

Unfortunately, as seductive as it is, this view of history, considering the various versions of the Ionic base as trials and errors leading to a product according to a preexisting program, is wrong. It is more correct to say that, as the rise of aesthetic awareness proceeded and as abstract analytical thinking and quantification developed, there were changes in the Ionic profile that manifested a growing awareness of a compositional approach to architecture and of the possibility, if not the potentials, of a rule-based formal architectural activity (see figures 58, 60, 61).

Turning again to the Attic base, it has also been combined with the plinth (see figure 59m). The reasons for such a new development are not known. We can see this new version in the Temple of Artemis at Magnesia (second century B.C.), carried out by the great Greek architect and theoretician Hermogenes, but also at the Temple of Fortuna Virilis beside the Tiber in Rome (figure 34) and the famous Maison Carrée at

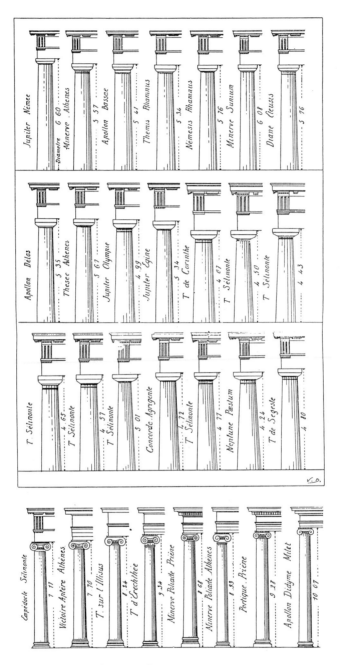

58. Comparison of Doric and
Ionic columns from antiquity
(Planat, undated (late nineteenth
century)).

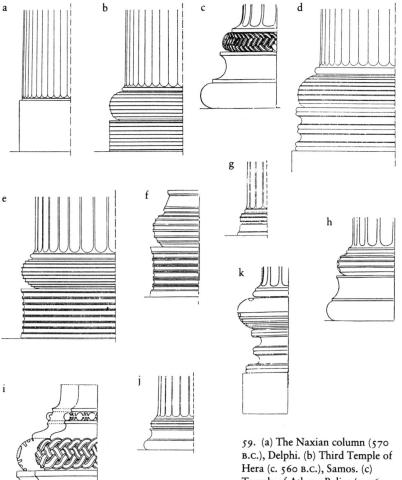

59. (a) The Naxian column (570 B.C.), Delphi. (b) Third Temple of Hera (c. 560 B.C.), Samos. (c) Temple of Athena Polias (c. 560 B.C.?), Athens. (d) The Arthemision (c. 550 B.C.), Ephesus. (e) Temple of Hera (c. 525 B.C. and later), Samos. (f) Temple of Hera (c. 525 B.C. and later), Samos. (g) The Athenian Treasury (478 B.C.), Delphi. (h) Temple by the Ilissos (450 B.C.), Athens. (i) Temple of Nemesis (c. 435 B.C.?), Rhamnos. (j) Erechtheion, east porch (c. 421–407 B.C. mainly). (k) Temple of Athena (c. 340 B.C.), Priene. (l) Temple of Apollo Delphinion (Hellenistic times), Miletos. (m) Propylaea of Appius Claudius (49 B.C.), Eleusis.

Plate 14.   Nº 15 Page 155.

BASES of Different COLUMNS.

DORICK.

Attick Bafe.   COLISÆUM.   VIGNOLE.
A.PALLADIO.

A.PALLADIO.   COLISÆUM.

IONICK.

Portico Pantheon.   Theatre of Marcellus.
CORINTHIAN   IONICK.

A Scale of Sixty Minutes,
or One Module.

P. Fourdrinier Sculp.

60. Ware (1768).

Plate 25

TUSCAN ORDER.

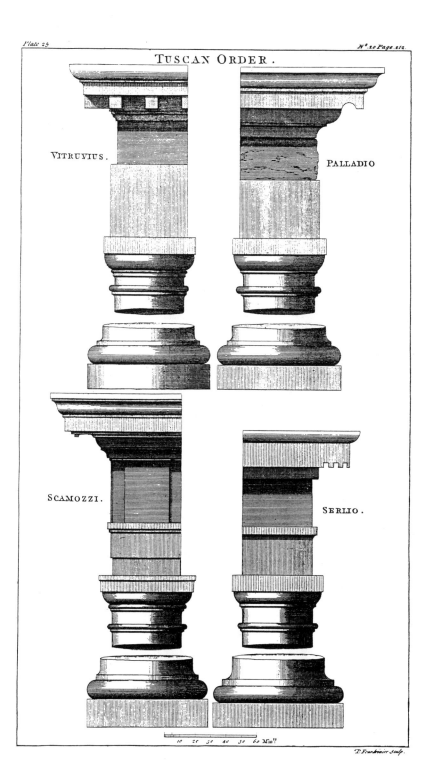

VITRUVIUS.

PALLADIO

SCAMOZZI.

SERLIO.

10   20   30   40   50   60 Min.

T. Fourdrinier sculp.

Plate 20   VARIATIONS in the DORIC ENTABLATURES. *N° 16 Page 165*

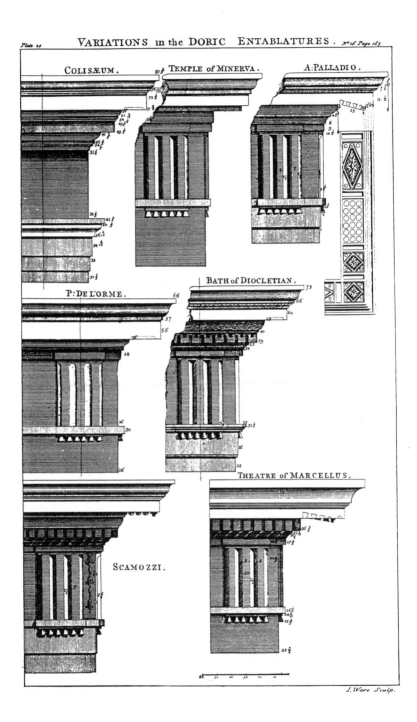

COLISÆUM.   TEMPLE of MINERVA.   A:PALLADIO.

P:DE L'ORME.   BATH of DIOCLETIAN.

THEATRE of MARCELLUS.

SCAMOZZI.

I. Ware Sculp.

61. Ware (1768).

Nîmes. Vitruvius, in fact, canonized this solution, which has led to its wide acceptance since the Renaissance (*De Architectura*, bk. I, ch. III, para. 1, 2; see figures 64, 65).

The introduction of this fourth element, the plinth, does not seem to disturb the schema of tripartition. The plinth can be seen formally as part of the crepidoma or the pedestal, as we have already suggested in the case of the so-called Asiatic base. If ambiguity is tolerated, then one can be happy with this alternative base, leaving the Erechtheion profile as the unambiguous conception.

Some approaches to architectural composition—De Stijl, for instance—exclude the idea of hierarchy and of ranked compositional elements; they also eliminate ornaments and contour patterns. Their problematic program to explore and use space is different from that of classicism, and they arrive at different results. Still other approaches, such as expressionism, aspire to contour patterning as almost the single instrument for creating architectural form. These approaches defy taxis, avoid the elementariness of architecture, abandon genera, and declare themselves above the ruling of metric patterns. They try to develop walls, openings, complete plans exclusively out of the very stuff of their ornaments and their contour shape units. They rely on the adventures of the profile, and they also arrive at products quite different from the classical buildings. These are poetics as coherent as the one of classicism and equally complex to talk about in any detail. To do a proper job analyzing such anticlassical poetics is an altogether different enterprise from the one we have undertaken here.

Classical architecture applies contour patterns, or ornaments, in a limited and systematic manner. Its purpose is mainly to give shape to the members of the genera and, through them, to an architectural scale to form a sense of architectural modality and the possibility of a gradational system of hierarchical composition. Once this is done and once there is a pattern ordered by taxis, the rest is taken care of by metric patterning, what is known in classical poetics as symmetry.

3 Symmetry: The Relations

Up to this point we have discussed taxis and the genera, two of the three levels of composition that go into the poetics of classical architecture. We now enter the third, symmetry, and with this we complete the general presentation of the classical canon.

Once a building has been divided through taxis and once a set of genus elements have been chosen, the next step is to place the elements inside the divisions. Symmetry tells us how to do this. In this sense, it covers all kinds of relations between architectural elements. It means more than just the perfect correspondence between elements with respect to a given line or plane—in other words more than what is usually called *bilateral symmetry*. Symmetry in the broad sense we use here also means more than commensurability of elements—a sense that the term incidentally assumes most of the time in Vitruvius's *De Architectura* and which we have already discussed in reference to the genera as *proportionality*.

Here, symmetry is used to cover universally all constraints of architectural composition that refer to how elements are chosen and placed in relation both to one another and to the overall structure of taxis. There are two kinds of relations in the composition level of symmetry, two schemata: one determined by *rhythm* and one, to borrow a term from classical rhetoric or music, governed by architectural *figures*, either *overt* or *subtle*.

RHYTHM

Rhythm is one of the most fundamental formal means of composition in classical music, poetry, and architecture. In architecture particularly it is a basic device for creating a building as a world within the world. Repetition, or periodic alternation of compositional units, makes the work stand out in relation to the amorphous random spaces that characterize the surrounding world. Rhythm employs stress, contrast, reiteration, and grouping in architectural elements. By using these aspects of formal organization, *metric patterns* emerge. These are small, simple standard groups of stressed units joined to unstressed ones and repeated regularly within a given division of taxis. Metric patterns constrain the position of architectural elements in a building, relative to each other.

Stress is based on the distinction between strong and weak architectural elements, the difference being conceptual rather than of a visual sensation. When we say that an element is stressed or unstressed, we mean that a unit of the composition has a formal meaning and not that it hits our eyes in a certain way. Not that rhythm is unconnected to the material reality of the building and to the function of its elements as light sources. These visual data are fundamental, but they have to be interpreted within a conceptual framework in order to acquire formal meaning. The same is true about perceiving the assemblage of stressed and unstressed elements. Relative distance between the elements plays an important role in forming such groups (see figure 62), but distance should not be taken as a real measure. It is associated only with space.

The force of the beat, the stressed architectural element, and the number of intervals between the beats, the unstressed elements, produce metric units and metric patterns that control the distribution of accentuation in space. In the most familiar example of classical architecture, that of a portico or a front of a temple (see figure 63), the most elementary kind of metric pattern appears to be that of the column, an accentuated element followed by an intercolumn space, a nonaccentuated element (see figures 62, 64). This is the "trochaic foot" of the architectural poetics—the stressed element followed by the unstressed interval. Metric patterns distinguish the kinds of temples by reference to the number of columns contained in the colonnade (see figure 67): *tetrastyle* for the temple with four columns, *hexastyle* with six, *octastyle* with eight, *decastyle* with ten, and *dodecastyle* with twelve. With the disappearance of the temple type in modern times these names came to be associated with the porticoes that served as entrances to private and public buildings.

The *rhythm* of a colonnade is defined by the metric norms of inter-columniation, which specifies the distance between two adjacent columns. Usually in the literature of classical architecture, this distance is specified in terms relative to the diameter of the columns, measured at the lower part of the shafts, the *module* (see figure 62). The distance between two columns can be read as the mute repetition of the column module inside the interval (see figures 65, 66)—four times in the *areostyle* colonnade (knock, tot, tot, tot, tot, knock), three times in the *diastyle* (knock, tot, tot, tot, knock), once and a half in the *pycnostyle* (knock, tot, tot, knock). Metaphorically, intercolumniation relations might be seen as the ordered spacing between human bodies, or, even more, as the structure of the steps in a dance, the art from which according to Aristotle all rhythm is derived. Intervals count as much as the bodies themselves. *Eurythmos*—good rhythmic organization—is the character of a work that is successfully metrically patterned, according to Vitruvius (*De Architectura*, bk. I, ch. II, para. 3).

Metric patterns are to be found not only in colonnades but in any regular arrangement that manipulates architectural elements through the polarity of stressed and unstressed. We can substitute pier walls for columns and windows, doors, or niches for intervals. We can also replace columns with pilasters and intervals with wall surfaces. Finally, we can consider sculptures as stressed elements and as intervals, the background of the sky on which their silhouettes are projected.

In all these relations of rhythm we identify a regular span formed by stressed elements placed next to unstressed ones. We can generalize further by stating that stressed versus unstressed differentiation in the metric patterning of architecture can be generated by several kinds of polar formal oppositions (see figure 74): solid/void, concave/convex, flat/curved, protruding/sunken, polished/rough, color *x*/color *y*.

The smallest metric pattern consists of a stressed element combined with an unstressed one, the unstressed flanked by the two stressed ones. Such is the case of the simple portico or the arch. We can call such standard combinations of architectural elements grouped in metric patterns and repeated within the same work or a set of works *architectural*

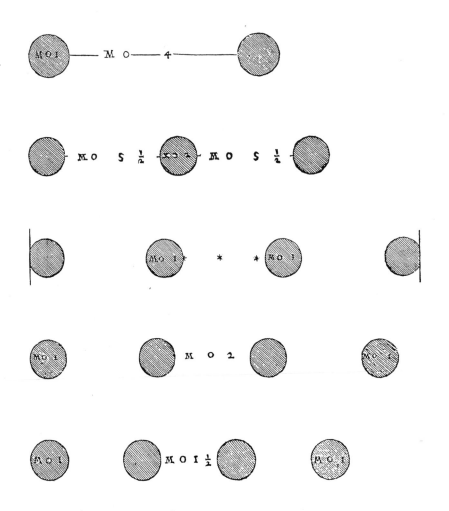

62. Intercolumniation patterns for
Tuscan, Doric, Ionic, Corinthian,
and Composite genera (Palladio
1570).

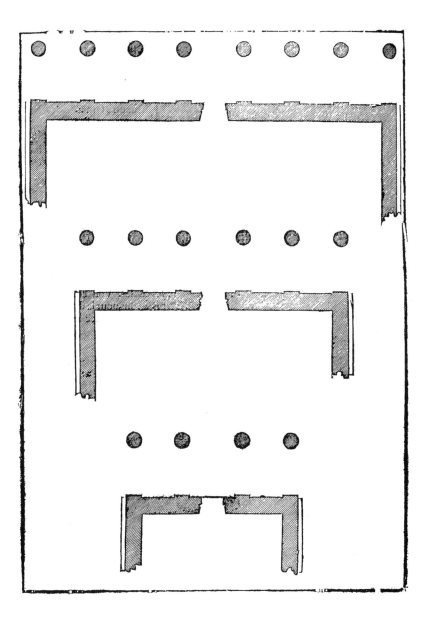

63. Tetrastyle, hexastyle, and octastyle patterns of intercolumniation
(Delorme 1561–1567).

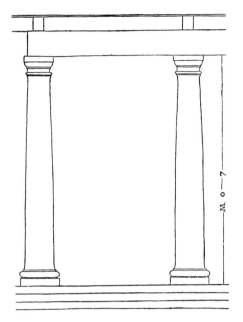

64. Intercolumniation patterns for
the five genera (Palladio 1570).

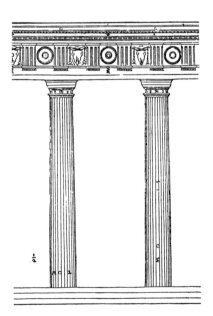

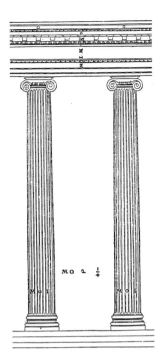

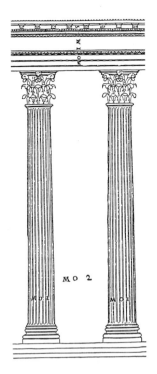

65. Intercolumniation patterns for Tuscan, Doric, Ionic, and Corinthian genera (Chambers 1791).

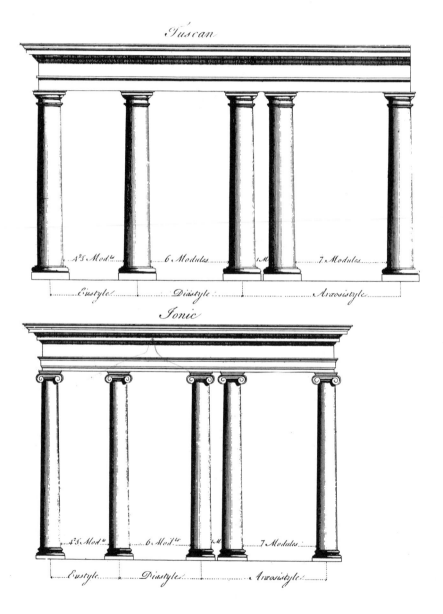

66. Picnostyle (a), diastyle (b), and
aerostyle (c) intercolumniation
patterns for Ionic and Corinthian
tetrastyle porticoes (Rusconi 1590).

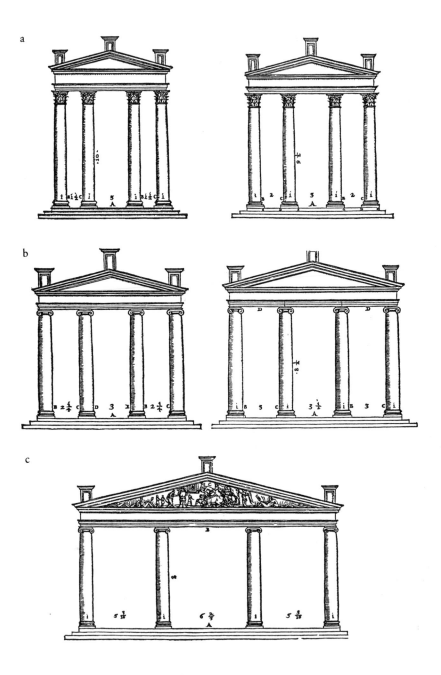

67. Octostyle, hexastyle, and tetrastyle patterns (Alberti 1726).

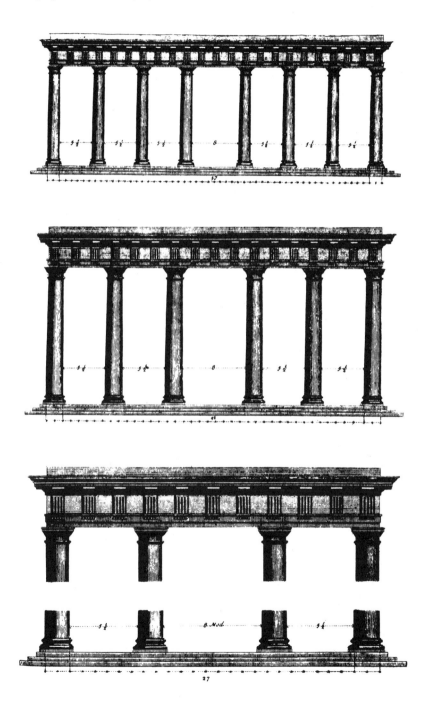

motives. There can be many more complex ones: the double column (see figure 71), the tabernacle (see figure 96), the tetrastyle portico (see figure 66), the arch framed by engaged columns or pilasters (see figure 68), the Serlian window (see figure 84).

Metric patterns can be developed in a linear succession or by following a regulatory line, which is straight or curved. Superimposition or succession of elements penetrating a building rarely leads to metric patterns. A different type of formal relation between elements is applied. Repetitions of an identical element are rare. Usually there are *modulations,* changes of the *genera,* of the modes employed.

The ancient Greeks were rather indifferent to such an idea. They did not hesitate to superimpose a Doric column on another Doric column or to have Doric columns used for both the exterior and the interior of the same building, only decreasing their size (see figure 69). In Hellenistic architecture modulation can be found in some buildings and later in the Roman Colosseum (see figure 70). Since the Renaissance, the Greek practice has become rare, giving way to the example of the Colosseum. Supercolumniation, or penetration of a building (see figures 71–73), is followed by modulation. This is carried out by applying the genera according to their ranking order, which we discussed in the previous chapter. Every floor of the building adopts an element, starting with the rusticated mode, continuing to a zone in the Doric mode, then to a zone of the Ionic genus, and finally to a Corinthian or Attic zone.

The same metric pattern or motive can be used repeatedly and exclusively, making up the whole of a composition; this is the case with a large number of facades of temples of antiquity and with more recent works such as many Renaissance facades cited by Percier and Fontaine (figure 167) and neo-Renaissance ones cited by Krafft and Ransonnette (figure 187). A metric pattern or a motive can also be used to form a part of an architectural composition, to be succeeded by a different one. Metric patterns also can be used in combination.

As interrelated elements from metric patterns and motives, metric patterns or motives can be conjoined to form larger architectural entities, phrases. Architectural phrases can in turn be linked to other phrases, generating larger compositional wholes. These complexes can be synthesized by simple *repetition* of the metric pattern or the motive. Sometimes, on the other hand, more-complex formal operations transform the initial unit by *modification* of some of its elements, as in the case of *double accentuation,* to terminate a phrase (see figures 79, 83). Typical modifications of elements are doubling the stressed element (see figures 84, 96); varying the size of the stressed element (see figure 86); replacing the stressed element, for example, the column by a pilaster (see figure 98); varying the size of the interval or of the unstressed element (see figure 80); inserting a new whole motive in place of an element (see figure 86); and inserting a protruding stressed element (see figure 82).

As elements are interrelated with metric patterns, metric patterns or motives can be combined with others in three manners: (1) one over the other (see figures 70–73), (2) one behind the other (see figure 74), or (3) one embedded in the other (see figure 73). Thus each metric pattern unit of one type might correspond to two or more units of another (see figures 74, 76). Metaphorically, one might speak of an accompaniment of a "slower," less articulated musical melody with a "faster," more articulated óne:

a   b   a   b   a
c   ded c   ded c

One of the most intriguing problems of classical architecture, intricately linked with the view that a building is a world within the world, emerges from the relation between metric pattern and taxis. Taxis sections the building and determines the limits of the evolution of a metric pattern. The pattern has to commence as well as terminate at the prescribed points. In classical music the problem of termination of a phrase or sentence, the so-called *cadence,* is also central to the fusion of taxis and symmetry, rhythmic and periodic schemata.

To manifest the idea of the boundary, the canon of classical architecture dictates that the termination element of a metric pattern should not only be stressed but *doubly* so. There are also other possibilities: making the previous unstressed unit longer, that is, "delaying" the accentuated termination, extending the section toward its ends; or the reverse, combining a shortening of the unstressed unit with a double stressing of the stressed unit, as in the celebrated *cadence* of Palladio's Basilica (figures 82, 84). There are many other strategies: doubling the size of the corner column to combine it with a pilaster; replacing the

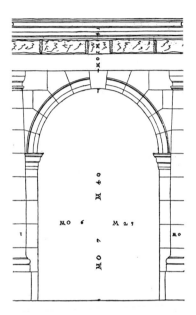
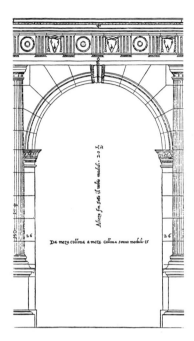

68. Genera applied to arches
flanked by pedimented columns
with entablature motifs (Palladio
1570).

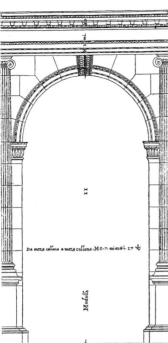

69. Temple of Poseidon in Paestum (Durm 1882).

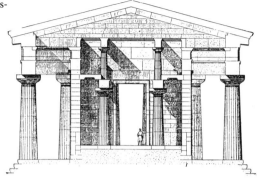

70. Superposition of the genera in the Colosseum in Rome by Palladio (in Barbaro 1556).

71. Superposition of the genera (Neufforge 1757–1780).

72. Intercolumniation and supercolumniation patterns applied to
the genera (Chambers 1791).

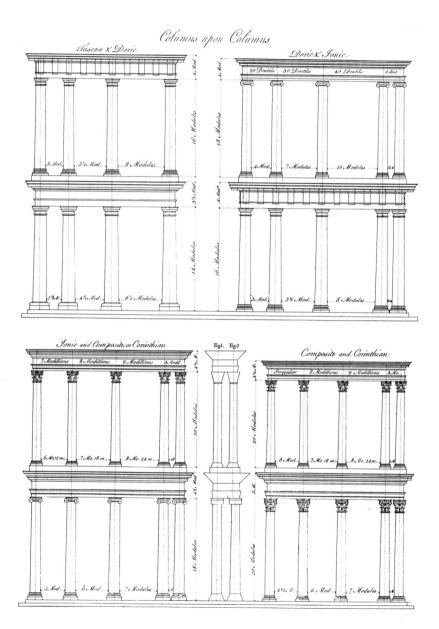

73. Superposition of arches
flanked by column motifs (Chambers 1791).

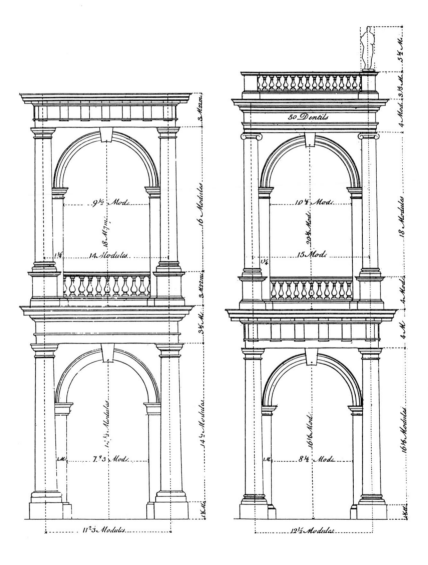

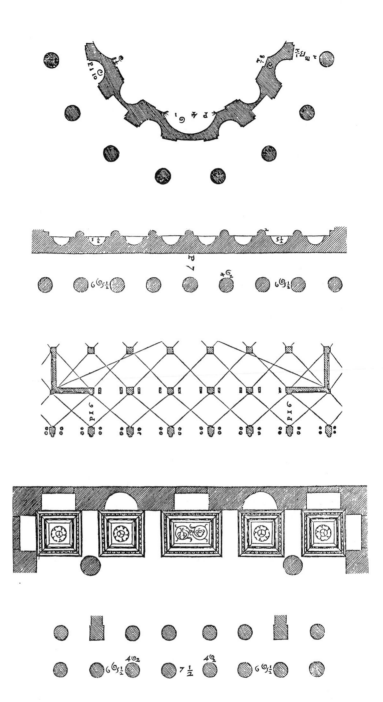

74. Succession of metric patterns,
one behind the other (Palladio
1570).

75. Temple of Antoninus and
Faustina. Sculptures as elements of
metric patterns (Palladio 1570).

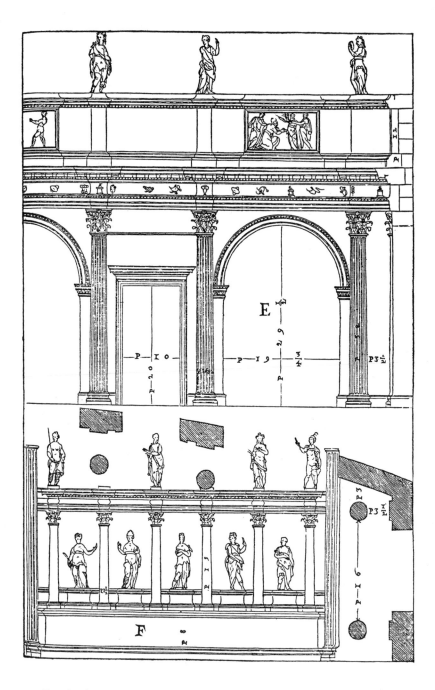

76. Temple of Nerva Trajanus.
Sculptures as elements of metric
patterns (Palladio 1570).

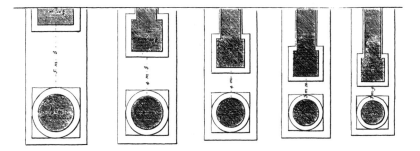

77. Relations between columns
and walls terminated by a pilaster
(Neufforge 1757–1780).

78. Relations between columns
and walls terminated by a pilaster
(Palladio 1570).

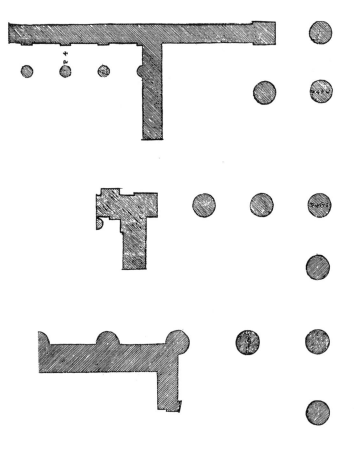

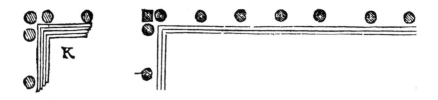

79. Termination pattern by accentuation (Palladio 1570).

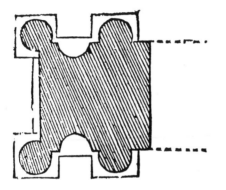

80. Termination by accentuation (Serlio 1619).

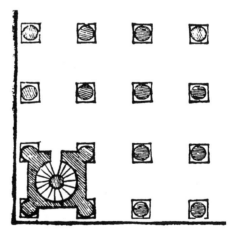

81. Termination by accentuation (Serlio 1619).

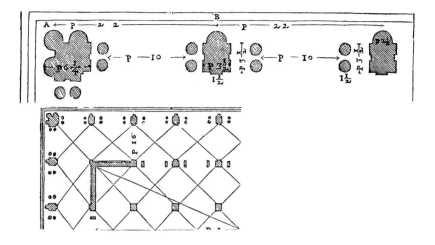

82. Termination by accentuation
(Palladio 1570).

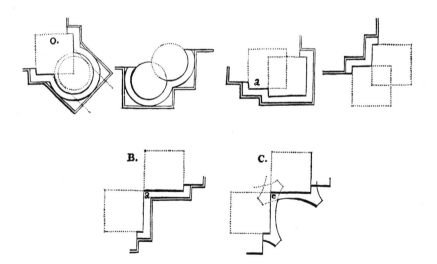

83. Termination by accentuation
(Blondel 1752–1756).

84. The Basilica of Vicenza, termination by accentuation (Palladio 1570).

85. Palazzo Chiericato, termination by accentuation (Palladio
1570).

86. Termination by accentuation
employing a wall section with an
embedded niche. Note the sharing
of the termination by two consecutive parts of the facade, or
Takterstickung. From Neufforge
(1757–1780).

87. Cornice soffit (Neufforge 1757–1780).

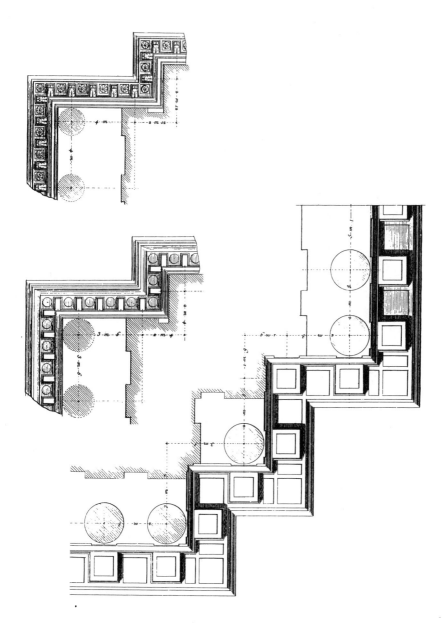

88. Corinthian soffit supported by
modillions (Pozzo 1693–1700).

89. Four examples of termination by accentuation (Pozzo 1693–1700).

round column with a square pillar; or multiplying the end member in more complex ways, as the intricate cadences of Pozzo suggest (see figure 89).

Just as architectural elements are distinguished as accentuated or nonaccentuated, so are the parts of the building, which also form patterns of accentuation or architectural phrases. The length and combination of such phrase patterns is controlled by the schemata of taxis. The taxis formula ABCBA, identified before as the most typical of classical architecture, defines an architectural composition made up of five parts, phrases, out of which these are stressed:

A C A

and two are not:

B B.

In these cases, the starting or terminating element of the starting or terminating part marks the boundaries of the particular part as well as the composition as a whole. Attention, therefore, must be paid to the way this stressing is carried out.

The end parts of the formula ABCBA are usually stressed, especially in larger complexes; so is the middle one. The Palladian villas, Villalpando's palatial Temple of Solomon, and the Louvre by Perrault are good examples of this pattern.

The stressing of a part is carried out through special formal operations that give a special marker to the part. Usually the volume of the stressed part is brought *forward* or made *taller,* or a unique feature, a pediment or a portico, is *attached* to it, a typical technique followed by Palladio (see figures 136, 137). In the facade of the Louvre, for example, Perrault stressed the center part by crowning it with a pediment and the end parts by inserting in them a triumphal arch motive (see figure 144).

A metric pattern is usually terminated by a stressed element, as in the case of the ABCBA phrase pattern formula in which a stressed part terminates the overall composition. On the other hand, the middle element in a metric pattern is most frequently an unstressed element—a door or a window, not a column or a pillar—the reverse of the ABCBA formula in which the middle part is stressed. It is interesting to note that, in this respect, the reasons given in classical literature of architecture tend to be anthropomorphic rather than formal. Vasari, for one, justifies placing the door in the middle of the lower part of the facade because in the human face that is where the mouth is.

FIGURES OF ARCHITECTURE

Under figures of architecture we include relations among elements or among their compositional units, such as parts, members, and details. Figures of architecture, like figures in rhetoric and music, are typified patterns for associating units in a manner that contributes to the completeness and wholeness of the work. And as in rhetoric and music, figures defy systematic classification. As a result, figures are mostly presented in the form of long lists. Despite their less than rigorous character, presenting classical composition more as a body of conventions than as a system, such lists have proven enormously popular. From the time of Aristotle's *Art of Rhetoric* and of the Alexandrian and Roman theoreticians of style to current studies on classical music, poetry, and architecture, such lists have kept appearing, for all their lapses in logical coherence.

This traditional lack of rigor in the classification of figures might indicate a weakness in the theoretical framework proposed. But it also might suggest that what we have is an open-ended set of constraints that can be superimposed on a composition, on top of the other constraints we have discussed—taxis, genera, and metric patterns—thereby increasing the layers of correspondence among the components of the work and multiplying the ties of interrelationships. Plainly, figures make the form of a building more complex and rich but with such an increase of overlapping relations that they also open it up to contradiction.

Let us proceed with the presentation of architectural figures. Borrowing from a classification system from two of the most influential classical treatises in history on the art of orating—the unattributed (but sometimes attributed to Cicero) *Ad Herennium* (bk. I, ch. IV, I) and Cicero's *De Inventione* (bk I, ch. XVII)—to architectural figures, we find two basic types of figures:

1. Those figures that make architectural elements interrelate in a way that *directly* and *overtly* contributes to the wholeness and completeness of the composition (parallelism, contrast, alignment, and analogy).

2. Those that do so through a *subtle* approach, by means of *insinuation* (aposiopesis, abruptio, epistrophe, oxymoron, "turning the corner," "feminine" cadenza, Takterstickung, and ellipse).

Overt Figures

Parallelism is an overt figure in which the architectural elements, parts, members, or details are inscribed in similar geometrical shapes and are placed in such a way in the composition that their corresponding constituent lines are *parallel* (see figure 90). If they are placed in such a way that these lines are in a right angle we have a figure of *contrast*. The diagrams by A. Thiersch (1889), which we include here, help to explain the workings of these two common figures of classical architecture (see figure 90). Close to parallelism comes *alignment,* which constrains the position of architectural elements by aligning their terminations or axes, as in the fantastic *enfilade* door patterns in French châteaus (see figures 144, 148, 165).

As we can see from the diagrams, all these figures use auxiliary lines, diagonal lines, limiting lines, and axes lines formally to control compositional units. These are called *regulating* lines (see figures 90–94).

Analogy is yet another architectural figure that overtly relates two or more elements or parts of a building by attaching to them the same feature in an equivalent position. Palladio, for example, placed a pediment on the portico and on the central part of the building. Similarly a pediment or a cornice or a pillar can be attached to many elements within the same facade. This is the case in the famous church facades by Palladio, in which analogy is employed in combination with parallelism (note the use of pediments and the framing of pedestals in the attic, portico, naves, aedicula, tabernacles, and to a lesser degree arches of the building) and with *alignment* (in Saint Giorgio Maggiore (figure 96), Saint Francesco della Vigna (figure 97), and especially in Il Redentore (figure 98)).

Overt figures apply layer on layer of formal structures, reinforcing conditions of consistency and completeness to the composition. Such an approach can be acceptable so long as, to cite *Ad Herennium,* our audience is "receptive, well-disposed and attentive" (bk. I, ch. IV, para. 6). But when "the case is difficult," when "doubts arise," and the audience is "alienated" or suspicious or simply worn out by too much exposure, then more indirect means are needed. Figures now contain contradictions manifestly, and they flaunt anomalies deliberately. But

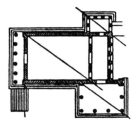

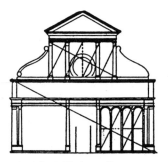

Erechtheion

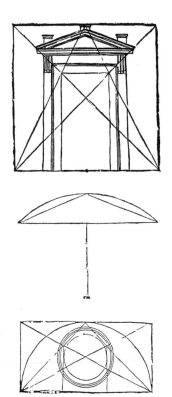

Santa Maria novella

91. Regulatory lines applied to a framed, pedimented door (Serlio 1619).

92. Regulatory lines applied to a portal flanked by columns and pedimented (Colonna 1546).

Cancelleria

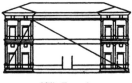

. Villa Farnesina

90. Parallelism and contrast figures (Thiersch 1889).

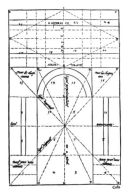

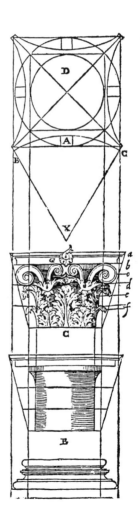

93. Regulatory lines applied to a
Corinthian column (Martin 1547).

94. Regulatory lines applied to a
Corinthian column (Serlio 1619).

95. Corinthian capitals with the
pattern of tripartition and with
the figures of parallelism and
alignment (Delorme 1576).

these disruptions of the consistency of the work are only "local" and apparent. Seen in the totality of the composition, they enforce the coherence of the work.

Subtle Figures

The image of order conveyed through subtle figures is not as immediately apparent as it is through overt ones. Instead of taking the path of simple, direct, unambiguous affirmation, subtle figures let appearances deceive, at least momentarily until their real function is revealed. They allow a seeming disorder, although in the end they reinforce order. With the subtle compositional device the intention is to create reversal, then recognition; deception, then a realization of the deception. This subterfuge is sometimes used to create tension and suspense.

Palladio's three celebrated church facades—Saint Francesco della Vigna (figure 97) (1562), Saint Giorgio Maggiore (1565; figure 96); and Il Redentore (1576–1577; figure 98)—give us the opportunity to examine three fascinating subtle figures of classical architecture that, borrowing terminology once more from classical rhetoric and music, we call *aposiopesis,* the interruption of a series (see *Ad Herennium,* bk. IV, ch. XXIX, para. 41; Quintilian 1970 [c. A.D. 70], bk. II, ch. IX, para. 54; Ratner 1980, p. 91); or *abruptio,* the breaking off of an element of a series; and *epistrophe,* the return to the initial series or element.

There is a clear tripartition division in these Palladian facades, a division that, compared with Rusconi facades, say, or any of the others we have seen before now, is much more extreme. There is also a bewildering discontinuity or aposiopesis between these divisions. The series of Corinthian columns or pilasters on the left first division that begins to be assembled in order to form a facade is interrupted by the middle division, a new series of giant Corinthian columns or pilasters soaring almost twice as high as the first. In the words of the author of the *Ad Herennium,* it is as if "something is said and the rest of what the speaker started is relinquished unfinished" (bk. IV, ch. XXIX, para. 41).

In the case of Saint Giorgio Maggiore (figure 96) the precise point of this breach of order is marked by an abruptio: half of the pediment, shaft, and capital of the last minor pilaster of the end division is incongruously affixed along the length of the half of the first major column or

96. Superposition of the overt and
subtle figures of analogy, alignment, aposiopesis, abruptio, and
epistrophe in the facade of Palladio's San Giorgio Maggiore.
From Bertotti-Scamozzi (1796).

97. Superposition of the overt and
subtle figures of analogy, alignment, aposiopesis, abruptio, and
epistrophe in the facade of Palladio's San Francesco della Vigna.
From Bertotti-Scamozzi (1796).

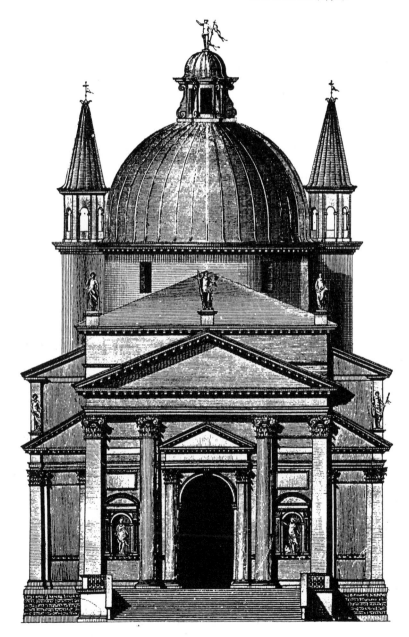

98. Superposition of the overt and subtle figures of analogy, alignment, aposiopesis, abruptio, and epistrophe in the facade of Palladio's Il Redentore. From Bertotti-Scamozzi (1796).

pilaster of the middle division. The new, giant series of columns or pilasters runs its course, as it were, forming a full tetrastyle unit. As soon as it ends, a half pilaster marks the epistrophe, or return to the first series of pilasters, which had started on the left. The third division is completed and, with it, order is restored.

Restored coherence is echoed through the reinforcing effect of the repeated tympana that crown not only pilasters but also the columniated tabernacles, entrance, and high attic in Saint Giorgio Maggiore and Il Redentore. Finally, unification is produced by the alignment of moldings across the entire facade at the level of architrave, pedestal, and bases of the tabernacles.

The three facades, then, are variations on the figures of abruptio, aposiopesis, and epistrophe. Many other interpretations have been applied to explain their irresistible attraction. Metaphors such as "collage," "interpenetration," and "transparency" have been used to bring the Palladian compositions closer to the contemporary sensibility and habits of design. But they are alien to the classical way of thinking. Other interpretations complement rather than conflict with the subtle figure interpretation. The facade of the Palazzo Valmarana (figure 99), for instance, combines a willingness to interact with the iconography of its urban context and the use of a subtle figure that we call *oxymoron*.

Oxymoron, even more than any of the preceding subtle figures, manifests contained anomaly, equivocalness, and the recognition of two apparently contradictory arguments as tacitly complementary. We turn again to Palladio. Once more, in his facade of the Palazzo Valmarana of 1565–1566, we have a *giant* or *colossal* mode. But this colonnade is in the Corinthian genus. Thus the most slender of the genera becomes the most dominant. The contradiction is manifested by setting a minor and a giant Corinthian colonnade next to each other. The overall effect is that of a parade of oddly virile adolescent girls. It is interesting that this mixture of aggressive and effeminate features was recommended for princely palaces only. But the suspense and adventure of contradiction, doubt, and recognition of the oxymoron are raised one level higher. At the termination of this building, where one would expect the most stressed component, such as a double giant Corinthian pilaster, one finds two superimposed elements, a caryatide atop a one-and-a-half Corinthian pilaster. Once more there is contradiction; the female, or at

99. Oxymoron figure in Palazzo
Valmarana (Palladio 1570).

least feminine, figure that one would expect to find on such a "feminine" base is replaced by a figure of a warrior, albeit a female one—Minerva in armor. But on the top of this train of inversions rests a giant Corinthian architrave, which, like the giant temple of the church facades we have just observed, restores the canon.

The oxymoron, like a witticism or a joke, is a contained violation of a norm, a provisional relief from an obligation that ultimately reinforces the rule and backs the coherence of the whole. It is a formal device that poets have been fond of since antiquity and that triumphs in the music of Haydn and Mozart. Oxymoron, like the other subtle architectural figures we have just discussed, seems to be undoing the idea of the classical edifice by pulling apart its agreement. Yet the effect is the opposite. There is a crucial state when figures seemingly cast off the intricate formal concatenations of classical architecture, through the structural displacement of an accent or a division, the unstressed termination, the elliptical motive, the decapitated member, the disrupted rhythmic grouping. But at the same instant there is the moment of recognition—the justification, reconciliation, and reconstitution of a strengthened canon.

We now turn to another famous example of classical architecture, if there can be anything more venerated—the Doric temple of antiquity. We discuss through this example another important subtle figure, which relates to metric pattern and termination. This figure is often referred to, superficially, as *"turning the corner."* Here we are faced with rules of composition that are as canonical as they are contradictory. On the one hand there is the obligation to terminate the temple colonnade pattern with a column, because it is a stressed element, and to align the stressed element of the triglyph with the vertical axis of this column. On the other hand there is the equally strong dictate that the triglyph terminate the frieze, which necessarily displaces the triglyph away from the central axis of the column below. This dilemma, which is by nature insurmountable, has been a thorn in the side of classical architects for centuries. The architects of Doric temples chose to go ahead and accept certain *local* anomalies: *Some* of the triglyphs do not fall over columns; *some* metric patterns are violated. But the first disturbance by these reversals is succeeded by suspense, a period of equivocalness, an *ambiguity* that results from the realization that columns and triglyphs shift, that both streams of colonnade and frieze continue to flow happily, meeting canonic obligations. We finally *recognize* the overall coherence restored (see figures 29, 100a, 100b).

A more detailed description of "turning the corner" would take too long for the present discussion. For those who want to see how the ancient Greek architects handled this case by manipulating intercolumniation, we recommend Robertson's (1971, pp. 106–111) eloquent description. More "straight" architects and theoreticians, such as Vitruvius (*De Architectura,* bk. IV, ch. III, para. 5), have been at a loss with this tolerance, the mixture of vigor and vice. They have censured the Doric temple for being too "faulty and incongruous," its defects "caused" by the constraints of "its symmetry," in the words of Vitruvius. Like other architects, for example, Arcesius, Pythius, and the great Hermogenes, Vitruvius ended up counseling against the Doric genus for temples in order to avoid what he saw as confusion. By means of a final compromise, he proposed keeping the triglyph above the column and the metric patterns intact but ending with an unstressed unit on the frieze, a half metope rather than a triglyph. In other words, he proposed an alternative termination, an alternative type of cadenza (see figures 25a, 100c). Once more we have a local anomaly that is overcome within the larger context of the work. In fact, we have another kind of subtle figure, which we can call *"feminine"* cadenza, borrowing the term from classical music theory (Lerdahl and Jackendoff 1983, p. 31). "Feminine" cadenza occurs when a composition terminates with an unstressed instead of a stressed element.

Let us continue now, with another figure—what in music is generally called *Takterstickung* (Ratner 1980, p. 38) and sometimes *overlap* (Lerdahl and Jackendoff 1983, p. 55). This subtle figure is close to "feminine" cadenza and "turning the corner" because it too involves a violation of the integrity of a unit of the composition. Here, however, the anomaly emerges out of the conceptual overlapping of two sections. The end of a part or an element is fused with the beginning of another. For instance, in the facade of Saint Sulpice in Paris, by Servandoni (1695–1757), both end and middle parts share a double column unit in the same way that the band crowning the lower level is at once the base of a superimposed one, as in a villa illustrated in Pain's *British Palladio* (see figure 151).

Ellipse, another subtle figure, has in common with Takterstickung, or

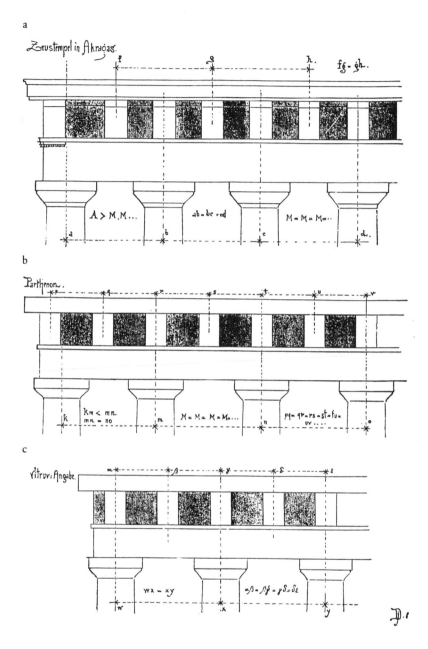

100. The termination of (a) the
Temple of Zeus in Acragas compared with that of (b) the Parthenon and (c) that favored by
Vitruvius (Durm 1882).

overlap, the abridgement of the complete structure of the classical composition. But, whereas in overlap the organization is cut short by extending one unit over the other, resulting in the two units becoming
one, in ellipse a unit is omitted altogether (Quintilian 1970 [c. A.D. 70],
bk. IX, ch. III, para. 58). What is also common to ellipse and overlap is
that the compositional structure, the formula, despite the removal of a
whole section, is not affected negatively. It is transformed without being
mutilated. The work implicitly contains the canon intact while it manifestly appears scissioned. An example of ellipse is in the facade of the
Palazzo Iseppo Porto, where the Ionic half-columns spring directly out
of an arched rustic ground floor to be immediately succeeded by a curt
Attic termination.

We have seen formal difficulties arise when overlaid metric patterns
have to be symmetrized in terms of stressed and unstressed units. Similar formal conflicts emerge when different shape patterns are collocated
and when profiles must harmonize with one another. Certainly this has
not frequently been the case in the temples of antiquity in their highly
minimal constitution, but it starts becoming an issue with the more
complicated buildings of the Roman empire, when elements of different
size and genus are intermixed, as in triumphal arches. This tendency
toward richer and more intricate combinations has continued to increase since the Renaissance. We frequently see columns of aediculae
flanked by taller columns, columnar arches framed by engaged columns
and entablature, or short and tall pilaster combinations, as in the much
favored Venetian window motif. To ignore this problem is to accept, as
one might say metaphorically, a polyphonic approach that tolerates
temporal incongruities. This is what Alberti did in the facade of St.
Andrea of Mantua of 1470, in which high and low, minor and giant
flanking elements bypass each other. As consciousness of requirements
of coherence increased in the sixteenth century, other practices appeared, such as keeping one element unarticulated while the other un-
folded according to the rule. This is the approach adopted by Palladio
in the Villa Pisani (figure 102), Palazzo Valmarana (figure 99), and the
Basilica of Vicenza and the proposed Basilica of Venice. There was yet
another path used to seize on these potential conflicts as excellent op-
portunities to generate a voluntary anomaly in order to promote a
subtle figure. An excellent case is to be found in the handling of the
details of the Villa Madama outside Rome, started by Raphael (c. 1516)

with Antonio da Sangallo the Elder and Giulio Romano and never really completed. Here, the contour movements of minor and giant Ionic bases embrace, so to speak. Flat plinths are forced into curved cyma reversa and cyma recta, plane dadoes into pulvinated ones (see figure 101).

The same is true of Palladio's Il Redentore in Venice (1567–1577; figures 98, 103). A minor and a giant column begin at the same point, that of the plinth of the base, and unfold, each in its own articulated manner. As in the Villa Madama, the two different profiles of the bases of Il Redentore rise, aligning contour movements at certain critical thresholds, such as at the beginning of a new section, producing extremely dissonant relations at other points. This creates an anomaly as intense and painful as the famous chromatic opening of the String Quartet in C major (K.465) of Mozart. But, as in Mozart's Quartet, as soon as the disjointed introduction is over, the piece rushes to confirm the classical canon; here the two shafts, minor and giant, surge unambiguously toward their respective ends. We pass from anomaly to ambiguity as the conjunct elements join in a larger, formal whole. All traces of ambiguity are finally overthrown when the two shafts, independent but *parallel* and *in analogy* to each other, meet with the two Corinthian minor and giant pediments crowned by tympana, equally parallel and in analogy. They embrace the whole. Finally. The triumph of coherence can be recognized as the surrounding and mounting tympana resound over the temple entrance, nave, aisles, and high attic in figures of parallelism, analogy, and alignment.

101. Raphael, Villa Madama.

102. Palladio, Villa Pisani, 1542–1545.

103. Palladio, Il Redentore.

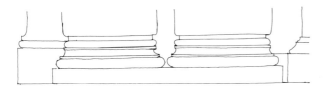

II ANTHOLOGY OF CLASSICAL WORKS

4 Architectural Scansion

The scope of this book is not historical. No attempt has been made to show the various stages of development of the classical canon. The anthology that follows is not historical either, although it respects chronology in the way it presents the works.

Beyond the utility of training in formal analysis and of acquiring formal architectural literacy, one might also find some intellectual pleasures in reading these plans and their well-measured forms. The reader is invited to go through the works with a pencil and paper as in an exercise of *scansion*. To some degree, therefore, the projects were selected because they provide good material for scansion. Originally, the term *scansion* applied to poetry. It means a method of examining verse foot by foot, of describing poetic rhythms through graphic notations for purposes of metrical analysis and study. In architecture we use the word metaphorically to connote going through the seemingly seamless plan of a building, point by point, in order to distinguish its morphological structure, to reveal and trace its implicit schemata, and to enjoy its formal quality.

The scansion of a building, like that of a poem or of a musical phrase, can lead to many interpretations. Many analytical pattern diagrams can be drawn from the same plan, assuming that the same formal schemata is at work in it and that the same view of classical architecture is in the mind of the viewer. The act of seeing, reading, and listening is not less equivocal than the act of conceiving. Each departs from the same formal schemata. Equivocalness in all cases emerges because the correspondence between canon and product, formal schemata and plans, is not simple and deterministic, a closed deductive system. The apparent autonomy of formal decisions and the intolerant world of fundamentalist formal abstraction that we have accepted as an analytical hypothesis, a methodological necessity, terminates here. In practice, one finds the world of forms tightly interlocked with other worlds: those of meaning, use, interest, and way of life, both personal and social. These worlds bias choice of formal pattern. In theoretical investigations involving the representation of the system of visual frames and formal schemata, one can maintain this tacit isolation of forms. One can also maintain it to some degree in the realm of formal games, but even here preference for a certain line of scission, a certain point of stress, a specific direction in rendition can come as the result of nonformal norms.

If, on the other hand, the unambiguous identification of a single correct pattern is an unrealizable goal, still something is gained— something that is sensed in the pleasure of playing again and again the formal games of conceiving and seeing, of drawing and reading classical plans, of laboring over the scansions of the works in this anthology. One conceives and sees forms through the frames and schemata of the canon, and there is a special hedonism in doing this. One begins to know more about what it is to know architecture, and this special gratification is the result of a second kind of knowledge, an intuitive one of a specific domain of the mind and of its workings.

Classical architecture, as we have seen, is based on formal conventions that can operate perfectly without being explicitly stated. Being able to design or see classical architecture is like being able to speak or understand a language; one joins a cultural tradition, a social universe. It implies the incorporation of formal conventions and the fitting of these conventions into a larger receiving structure in the mind. In real life, people are not shown the classical canon and all its levels and schemata. They simply come into contact with buildings, with events related to buildings, with representations of buildings and discussions about buildings. Only slowly is the canon and its schemata crystallized. One can design and see classical buildings felicitously; in other words, one can interact socially with them, conceive them, look at them, and talk about them, despite the fact that these canonic levels and schemata have never really been spelled out. They are tacitly nested in the building beheld. Bringing this implicit canon to the surface is not an easy matter. To start with, the definition of the classical canon, when it comes to many details, is subject to many versions and revisions. The idea of it as something frozen and monolithic is an abstraction toward which many have aimed but which has always remained elusive. The canon, in the mind of either the designer or the viewer of architecture, has many points that change, although they always depend on the context of the material of classical architecture that has been taken into account. The formal system of classical architecture has been a domain with blurred boundaries; the classical canon has been constantly modified, like any social convention. The classical building is an expression of this evolving canon that it confirms. At the same time it is the product and the creator of the canon. "The existing monuments," as T. S. Eliot (1953, p. 23) wrote in "Tradition and the Individual Talent," "form an ideal order among themselves" that is modified every time a new monument is introduced. "The existing order," continues Eliot, "is complete before the new work arrives; for order to persist after the supervision of novelty, the *whole* existing order must be, if ever so slightly, altered."

Like the boat of Theseus, the classical architectural canon undergoes a constant change of parts. Nevertheless, as in the boat of Theseus, the idea of order, the search through time for a work as a world free of contradiction, is preserved. For this reason the poetics of classical architecture must have as an indispensable part an anthology of works in addition to the exposition of the canon.

To use this anthology as a proper complementary part to that of formal analysis, one must keep in mind that the form of each plan is less important than the relation between plans. For this reason, the study of a series of plans is more revealing than the study of a single one. Thus, whenever it has been possible, we have reconstituted such series, respecting the integrity of the work of each author.

The plans of Cataneo must be read as a series. Special attention should be paid to how many simple mother taxis formulas are assembled to generate composite patterns and how these mother formulas on the way to being assembled have been transformed—how parts are fused and subtracted. The Cataneo series (figures 105–107) should be related to the series of plans by Durand (figures 165, 166). Are there any conclusions to be drawn about composite patterns and transformations from these examples. How do such conclusions stand if one takes into consideration the Serlio plans (figures 108, 109)?

We have already discussed the Serlio plans and his examples of rectangular and polar grid schemata hybrid plans and his *ars combinatoria*. One can relate this type of combinatorics with the one presented by the Du Cerceau series (figures 120–123), in which individual units, themselves derived from the mother taxis formula of Cesariano, mostly by suppression of parts, are assembled and rotated, providing another kind of composite patterning. One can further compare with Du Cerceau (see figure 120a), Ledoux (see figure 162b), and Peyre (see figure 161) the way Serlio developed his hybrid patterns. Do these patterns differ in the way they were developed? In the series of plans by Ledoux (figures 162, 163) it might be interesting to identify the concatenation of pattern from space motive to spatial phrase and from phrase to sentence and section and then to examine these vast size cases in which the Cesariano mother formula has been used: Villalpando's Temple of Solomon (figures 140, 141), the Escorial (figure 142) and the Louvre plans (figures 143, 144), or even Versailles (figure 148). Does a pattern of embedding come about? How does the termination symmetry schema apply to the Percier palace and the Fontaine palace facades (figure 167) or to the superposition of rhythmic patterning? Can one draw some general conclusions about the treatment of form here?

These are certainly only some of the many exercises that can be carried out to connect what was discussed theoretically in part I with the plans presented here. The amateur of classical architecture should proceed by looking at the three levels of formal composition together to find out how they reinforce or contain each other and to develop a higher overview of the pieces of the classical canon put into action as an integral system. One should search for conflicts, exceptions, ambiguities. Does the system explain them? Does it excuse them? Is it the fault of the system or of the example, or should one simply tolerate this point and move ahead to another problem?

To read this anthology and determine the quantities, weights and intervals, and differences and similarities that manifest taxis, genera, and symmetry is to observe specific instances of unfolding canon and evidence of the continuous quest for order. It is to see classical architecture as a way of thinking, not so much of individual configurations as of general formal frames and schemata. It is to think about the mind, and, as we discuss in the next section, it is to think about society.

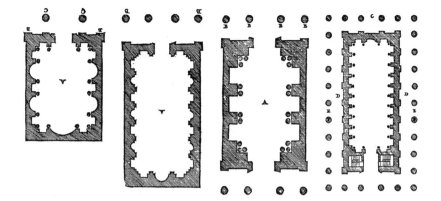

104. Rusconi (1590).

105. Cataneo (1554).

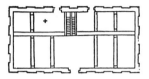

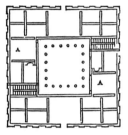

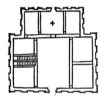

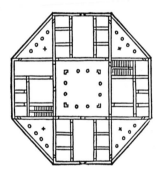

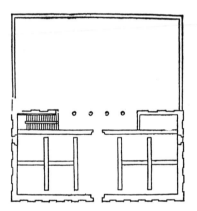

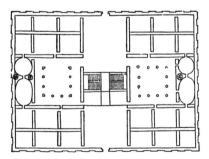

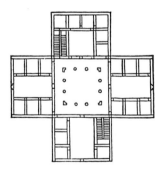

106. Cataneo (1554).

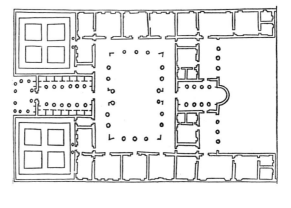

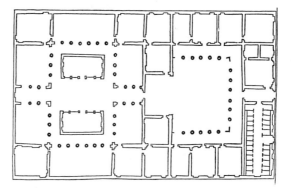

107. Cataneo (1554).

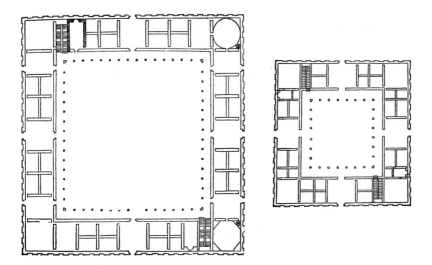

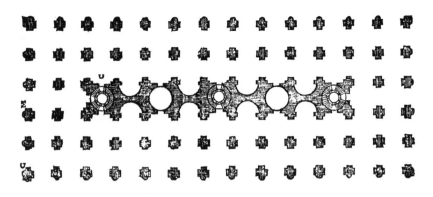

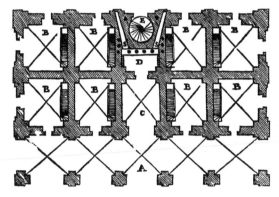

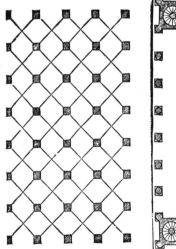

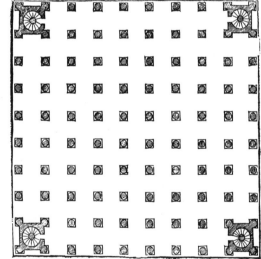

108. Serlio (1619).

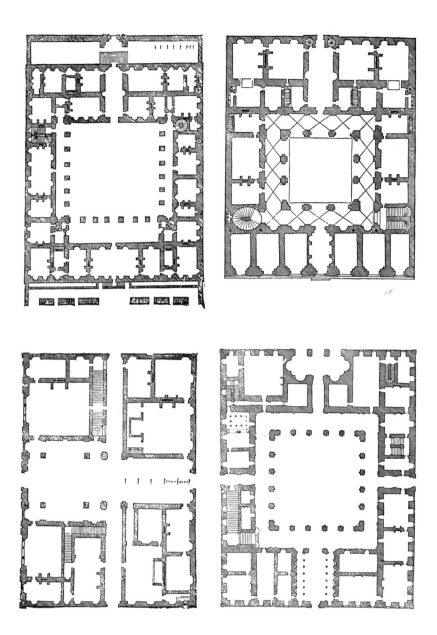

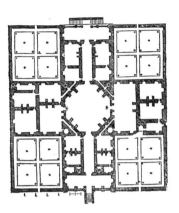

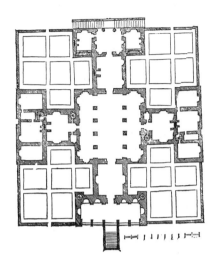

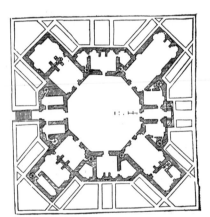

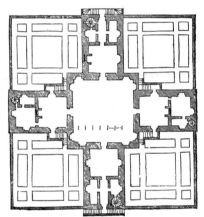

109. Serlio (1619).

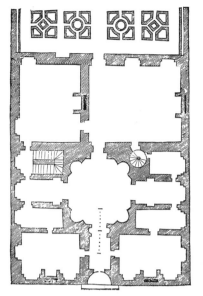 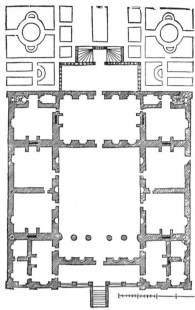

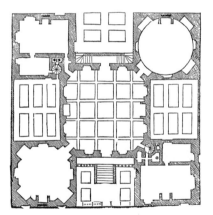 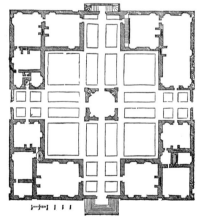

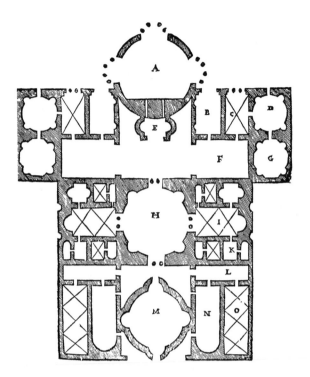

110. Baths of Titus (Serlio 1619).

111. Saint Peter's (Bramante) (Serlio 1619).

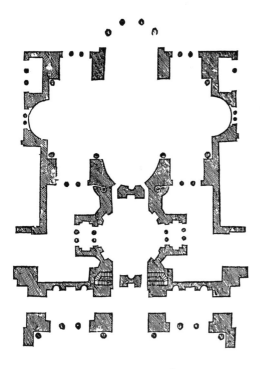

112. Baths of Diocletian (Serlio 1619).

113. San Pietro in Montorio (Bramante) (Serlio 1619).

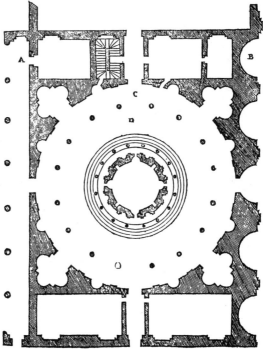

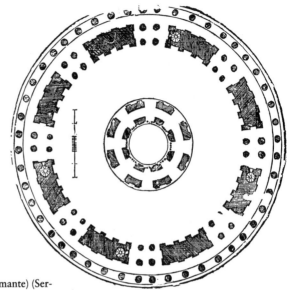

114. Saint Peter's (Bramante) (Serlio 1619).

115. Example of a round temple (Serlio 1619).

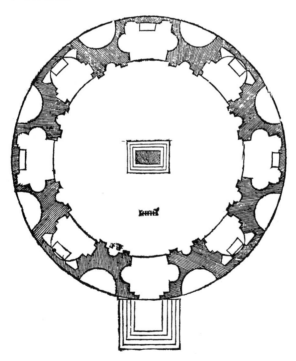

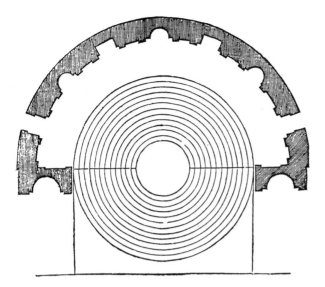

116. The Vatican Belvedere (Serlio
1619).

117. Temple of Bacchus (Serlio
1619).

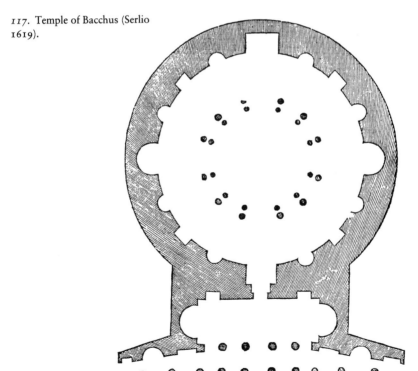

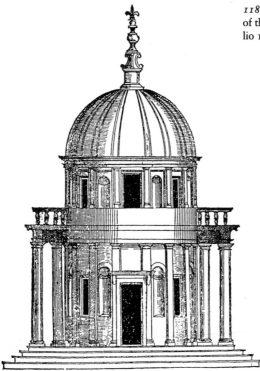

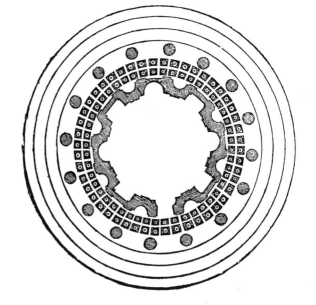

118. The facade and ground plan of the Tempietto (Bramante) (Serlio 1619).

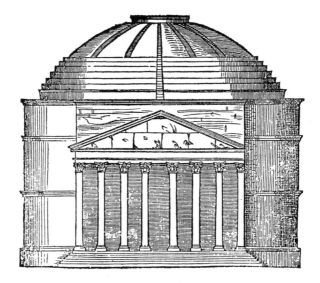

119. The facade and ground plan of the Pantheon in Rome (Serlio 1619).

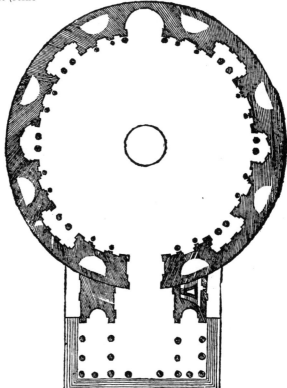

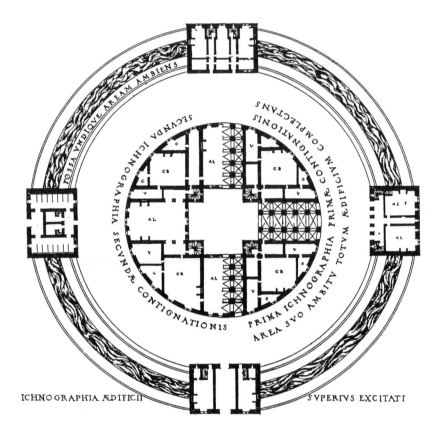

ICHNOGRAPHIA ÆDIFICII

SVPERIVS EXCITATI

120. Du Cerceau (1559).

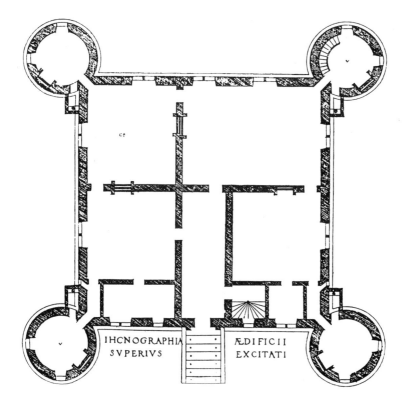

IHCNOGRAPHIA ÆDIFICII
SVPERIVS EXCITATI

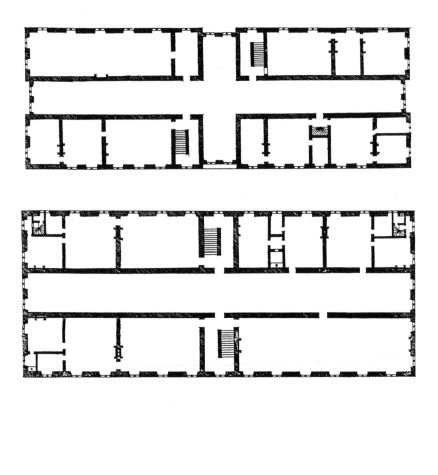

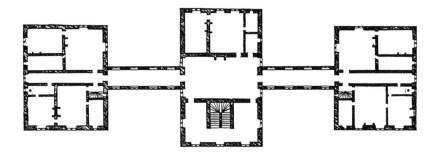

121. Du Cerceau (1559).

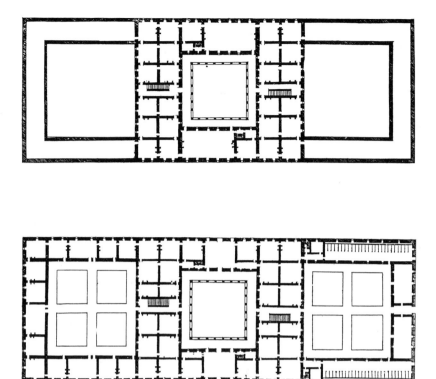

122. Du Cerceau (1559).

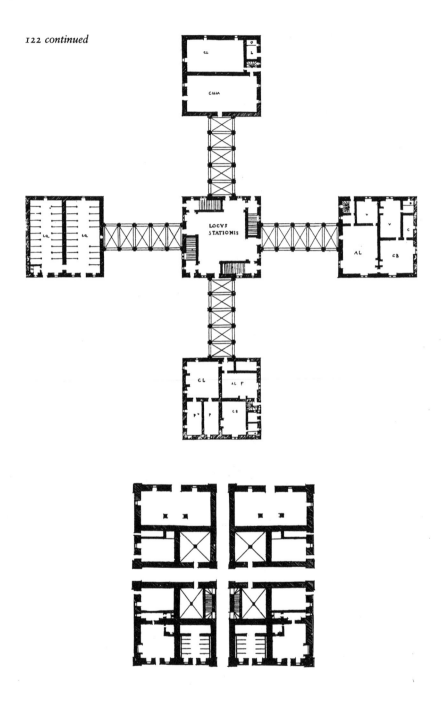

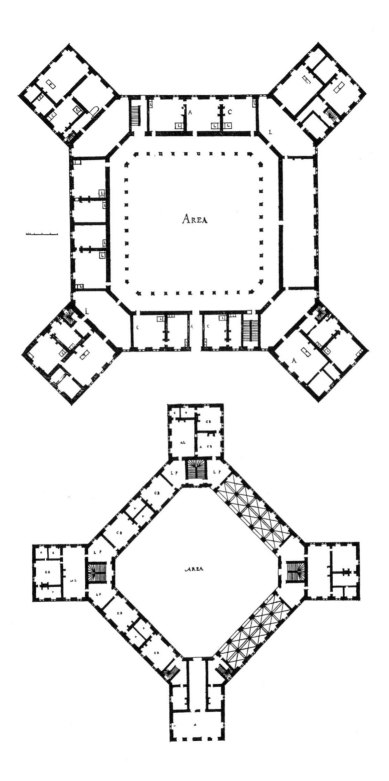

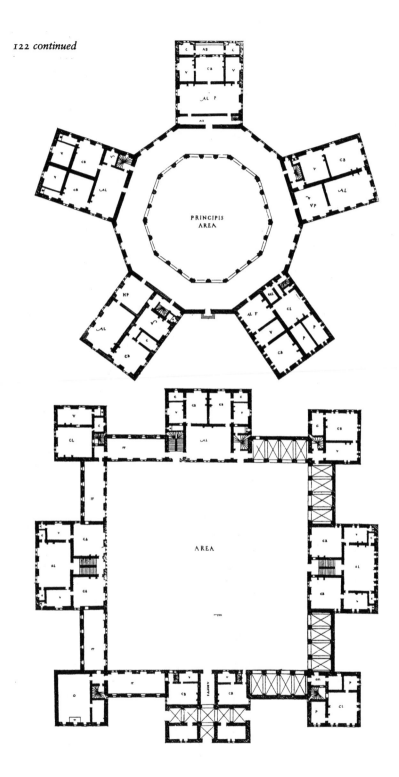

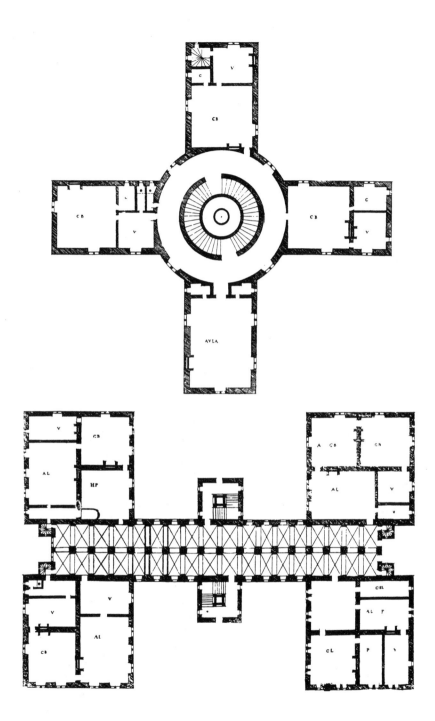

123. Du Cerceau (1559).

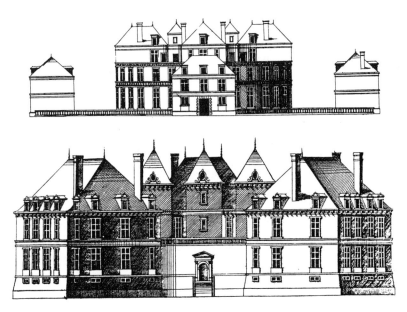

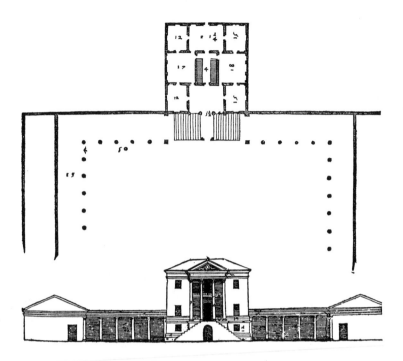

124. Villa Ragona (Palladio 1570).

125. Villa Foscari (Palladio 1570).

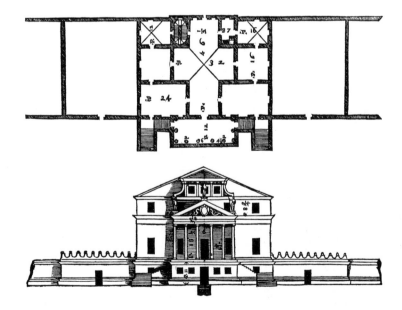

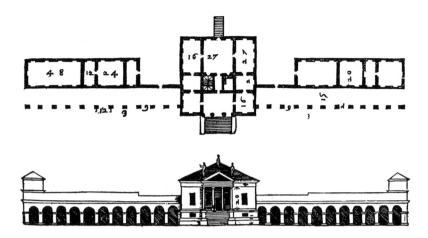

126. Villa Erno (Palladio 1570).

127. Villa Marco e Pisani (Palladio 1570).

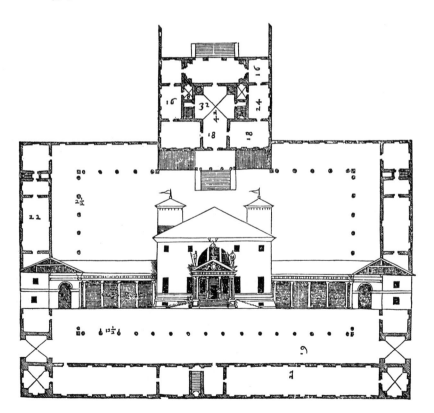

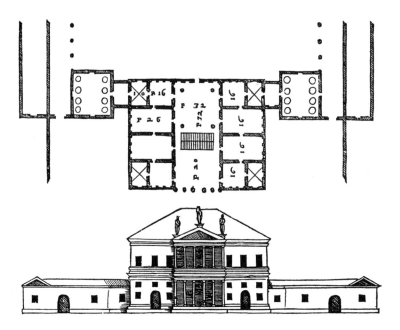

128. Villa Mocenico (Marocco)
(Palladio 1570).

129. Villa Pogliana (Palladio
1570).

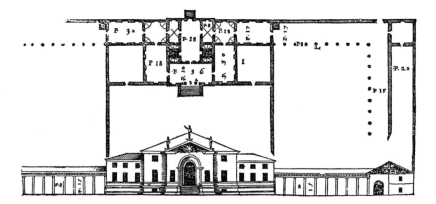

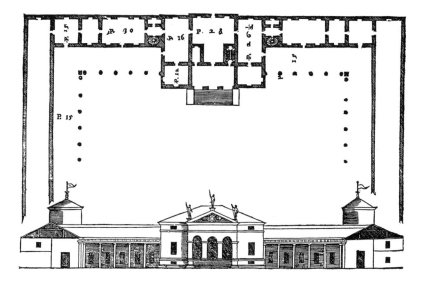

130. Villa Sarraceno (Palladio 1570).

131. Villa Thiene (Palladio 1570).

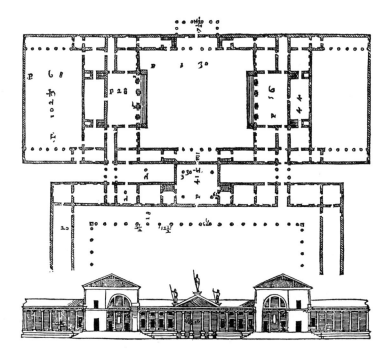

132. Villa Godi (Palladio 1570).

133. Villa Zeno (Palladio 1570).

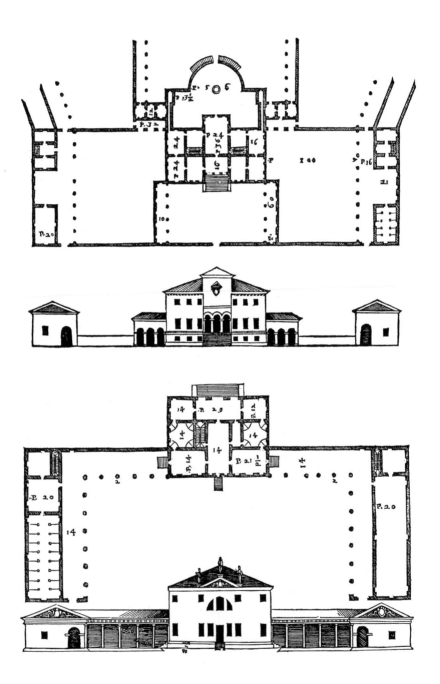

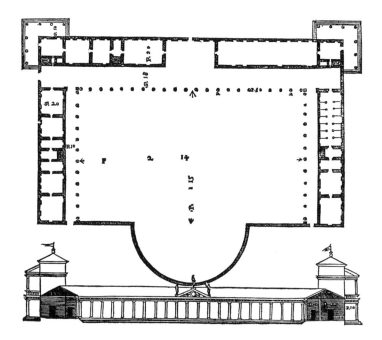

134. Villa Repeta (Palladio 1570).

135. Villa Badoero (Palladio
1570).

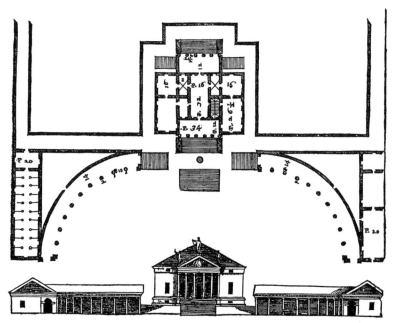

136. Villa Mocenico (Palladio
1570).

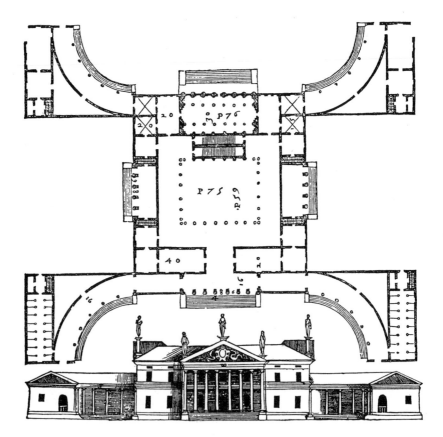

137. Villa Aquileia e Barbari (Palladio 1570).

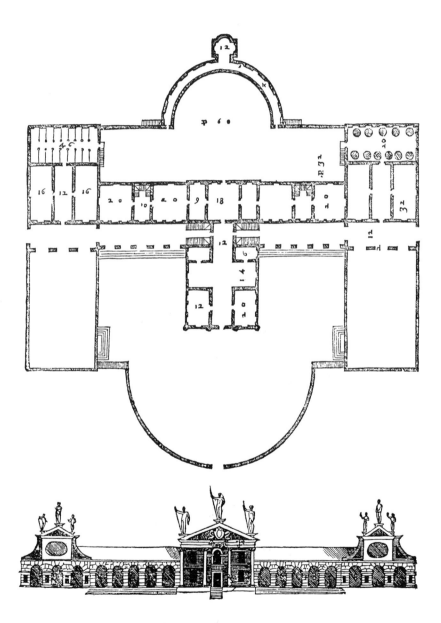

138. Villa Trissini (Palladio 1570).

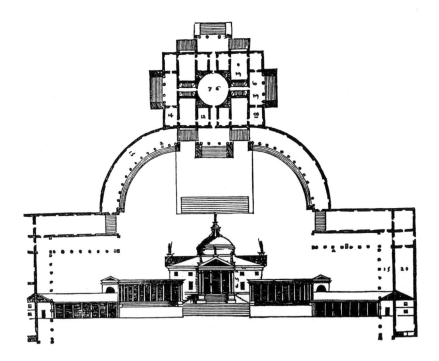

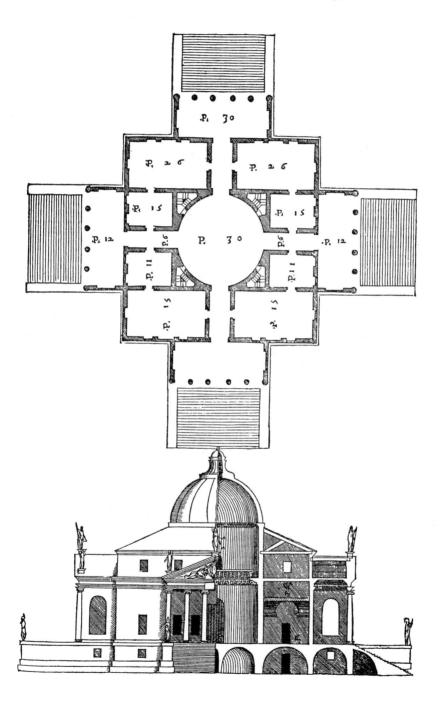

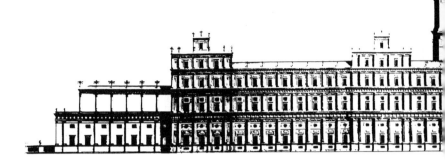

140. The facade of the Temple of
Solomon (Villalpando 1596).

141. The ground plan of the Temple of Solomon (Villalpando
1596).

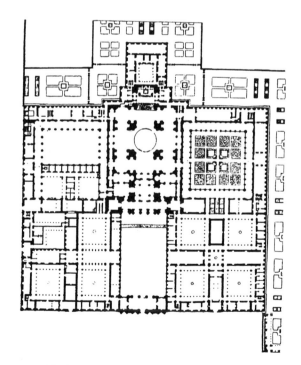

142. The facade and ground plan
of the Escorial (Villalpando 1596).

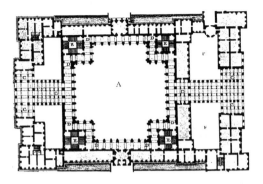

143. The Louvre, Bernini's project (Blondel 1752–1756).

144. The Louvre, Perrault's project (Patte 1769).

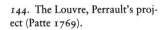

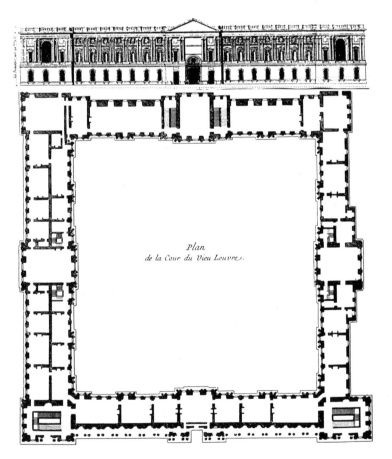

Plan
de la Cour du Vieu Louvre.

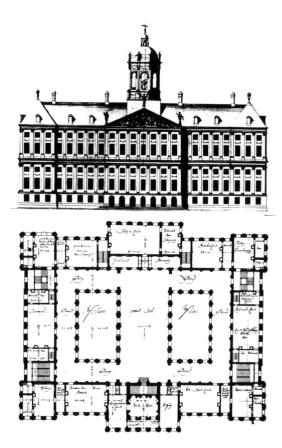

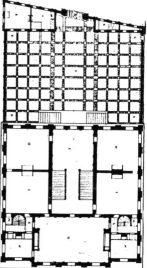

145. Amsterdam, the Palace (Campen 1661).

146. The Mauritzhuis in The Hague (Campen 1661).

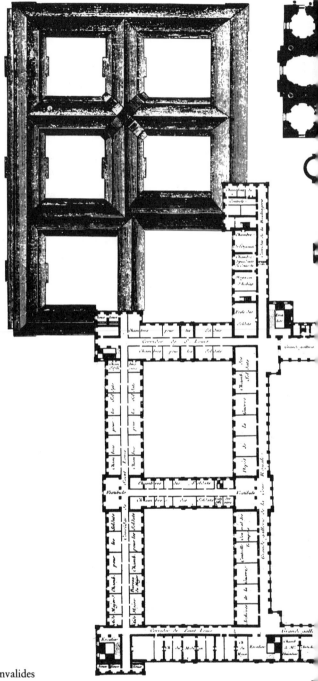

147. Hôtel Royal des Invalides
(Blondel 1752–1756).

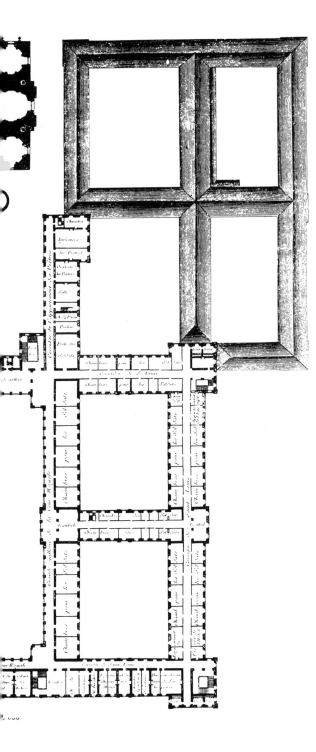

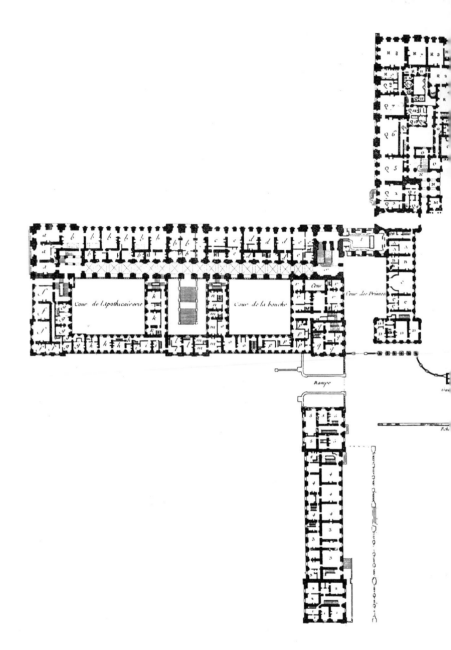

148. Versailles (Blondel 1752–
1756).

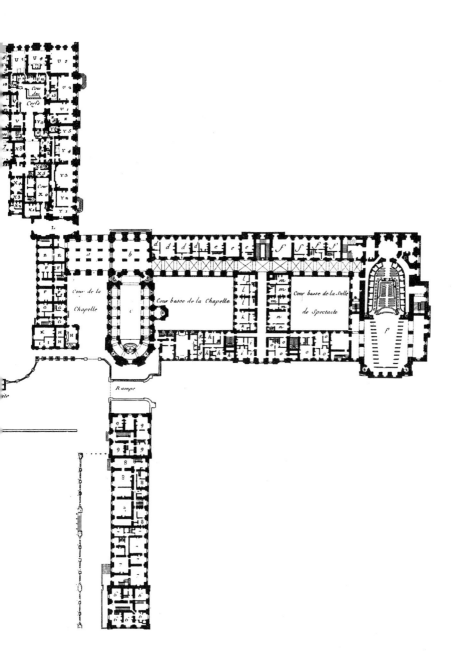

149. Morris (1750).

150. The facade of Saint Sulpice. Example of Takterstickung (Blondel 1752–1756).

151. Pain (1786).

152. Gibbs (1728).

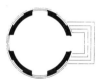
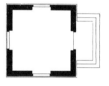
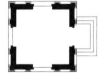

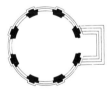
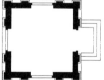
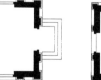

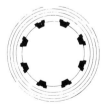
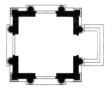

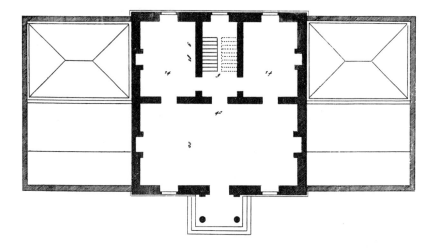

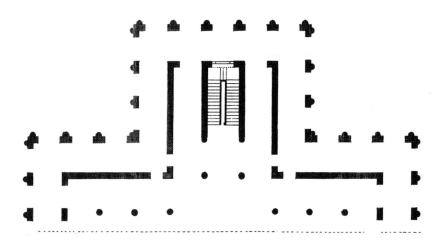

153. Gibbs (1728).

154. Morris (1750).

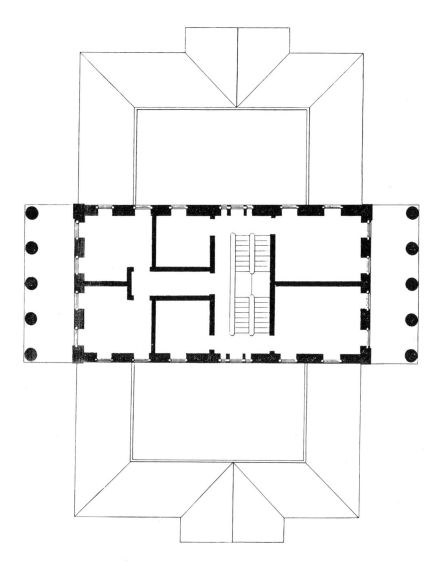

155. Lafever (1833).

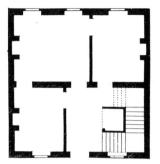

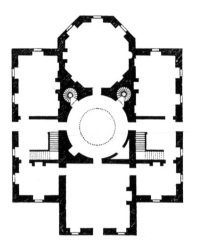

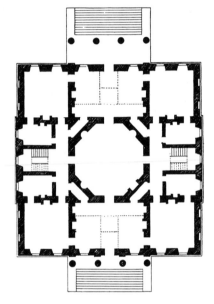

156. Morris (1750).

157. Gibbs (1728).

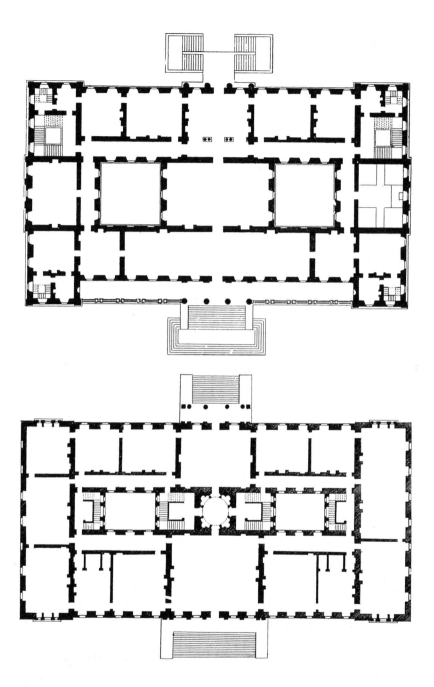

158. Gibbs (1728).

159. Morris (1750).

160. Hotel of M. Croisat, Place
Vendôme, Paris (Blondel 1752–
1756).

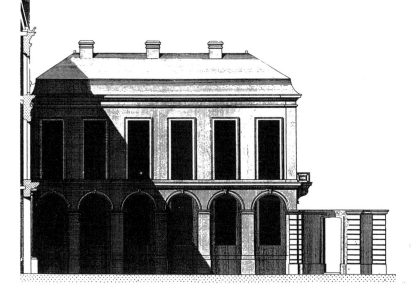

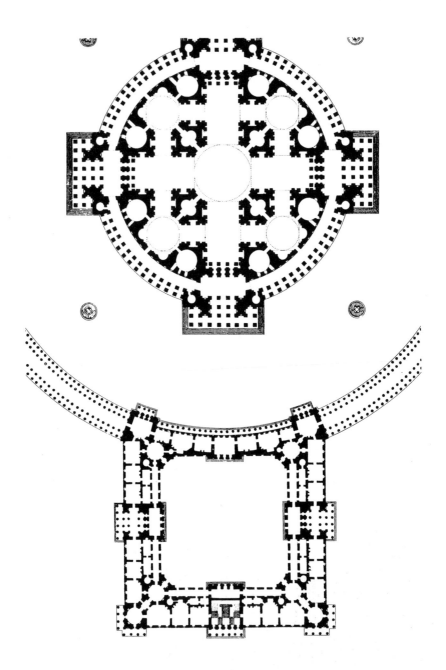

161. Peyre (1765).

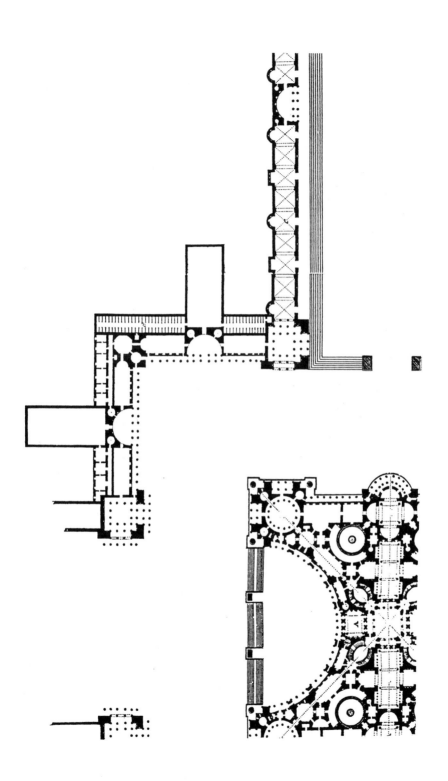

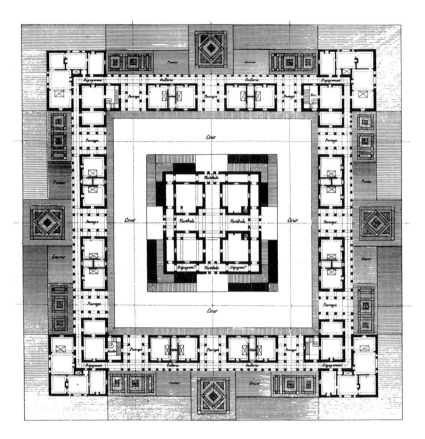

162. Ledoux (1804).

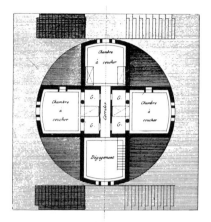

Rez-de-Chaussée

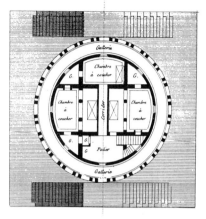

Premier étage

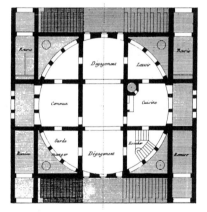

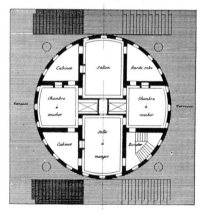

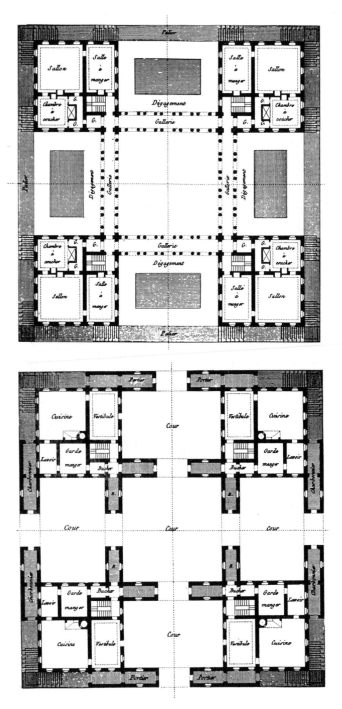

163. Ledoux (1804).

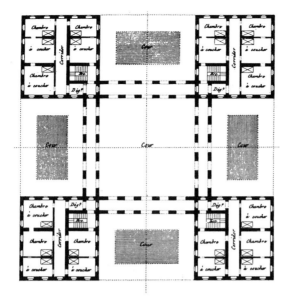

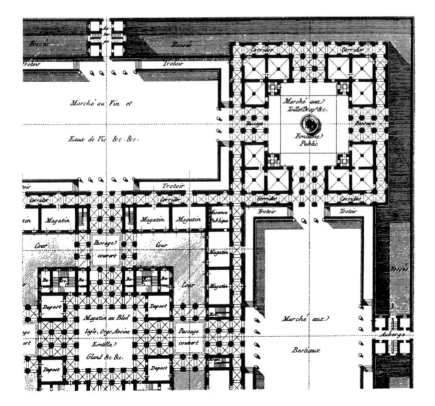

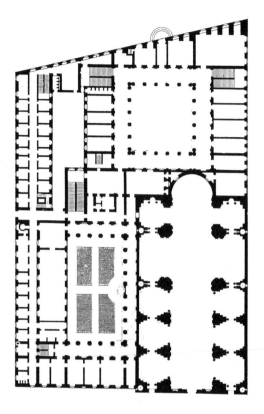

164. Ground plan of the Church of St. Ignatius (Percier and Fontaine 1798).

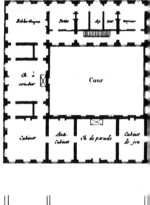

165. Durand (1802–1805).

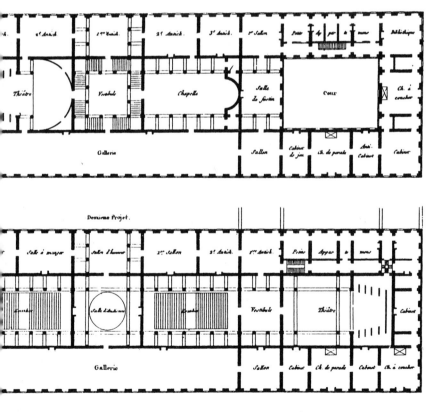

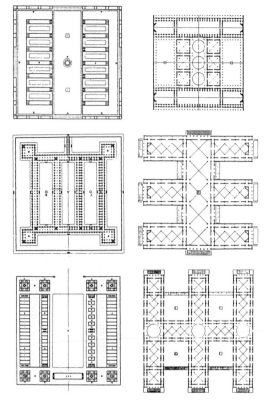

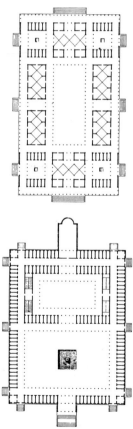

166. Durand (1802–1805).

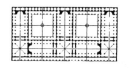

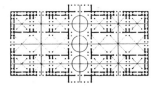

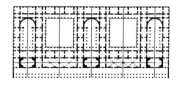

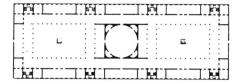

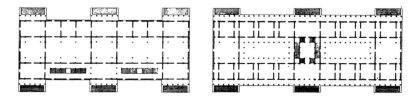

167. (a) Palazzo Sachetti. (b) Collegio della Sapienza. (c) Palazzo Ruspoli. (d) Palais Giraud. (e) Palazzo Farnese. (f) Papal Palazzo on the Monte Cavallo. All from Percier and Fontaine (1798).

a

b

c

d

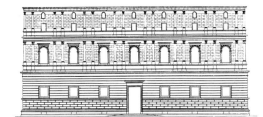

e

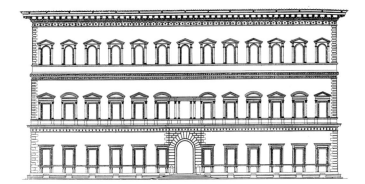

f

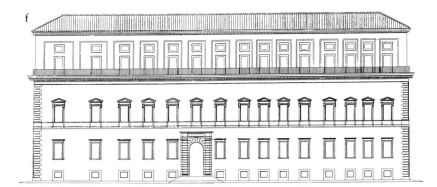

168. Krafft and Ransonnette
(1801–1802).

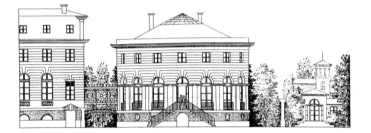

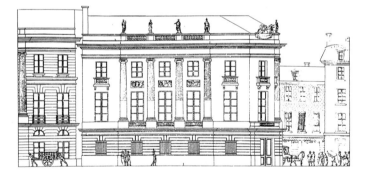

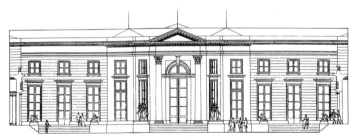

169. Krafft and Ransonnette
(1801–1802).

170. Krafft and Ransonnette
(1801–1802).

171. Krafft and Ransonnette
(1801–1802).

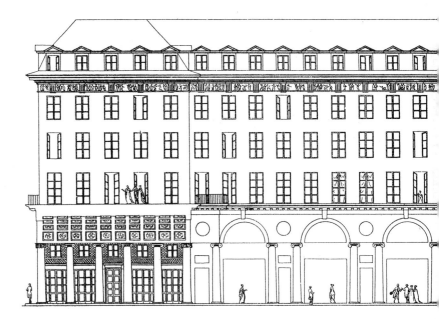

5 Parataxis: The Architectural Parade

The preceding anthology included projects whose classical logic was, on the whole, overwhelmingly clear. This is because the works were assembled in order to demonstrate the feasibility of the classical system and its poetics of order.

This book could have ended at this point. Certainly classicism would have appeared all the more infallible and simple. But we are extending the presentation, and we are doing so not only to reveal the limits of the classical order but also to outline alternative directions that it has been forced to take because of them.

We start with the example of buildings that for some reason cannot stand free. They have to touch sides. This constraint is a significant obstacle for classical architecture, which expounds that a building is a world within the world, independent of outside conditions. In ancient Greece, temples turned a cold shoulder to every structure that happened to be next to them, even if this other structure was another temple. In order to accommodate the new constraint, new formal solutions were needed. These gave birth to a specific classical formula, which we call *parataxis*.

Parataxis is one of the most compelling of classical inventions. It connotes a kind of taxis, a schema for concatenating formal units. Each unit is part of a linear, consecutive cumulative whole with well-defined upper and lower limits but without specified side terminations. The original use of the term *parataxis* applied to a body of troops displayed ceremoniously, as in a procession or a parade. The metaphor of the "architectural parade" refers to the lateral coordination and coherent sequence commonly found in classical streets or squares and occasionally in long utilitarian buildings of the nineteenth century.

Parataxis usually emerges from the juxtaposition of individual town houses. It is generated by the assemblage of independent metric patterns created by the strictly aligned fronts of the houses, provided that the units permit horizontal continuities or modular interrelations. The front of each unit is most effective in forming such a cumulative impact when its metric patterns are brief and simple and when it avoids becoming a self-contained integral composition: Thus the accentuation of the ends of the unit can have a negative effect, as can the stressed centrality of the entry, especially if this stress takes the form of a portico crowned by a pediment. When the front of the unit is too fragmentary, it is equally difficult for a cumulative pattern to emerge and for parataxis to form.

There are almost no constraints with regard to the number of units. There are versions of street patterns in which the block is seen as a self-contained unit and the corner units are treated as beginning or end sections of a classical building composition. But this is not always the case. Like so-called free verse in poetry, this pattern draws its coherence from an apparent metric unity that, when carefully measured, is found to be lacking by far the regularity of a periodic distribution of stressed and unstressed parts. But as in free verse, when metric anomalies appear in these street patterns, their effect is minor.

Parataxis is more permissive and more tolerant than any of the other formal schemas of classicism. Anomalies are treated as episodes whose justification remains in suspense. The continuous unfolding of metric themes and architectural phrases imply that somewhere in the next group of units there will be a counteracting pattern, a theme or phrase responding to the incongruity and, ultimately, explaining and permitting it. But the stream of metric patterns erases whatever unfelicitousness crosses its path, setting up new unresolved formal situations while concurrently bringing in new expectations of justification. Such strings of architectural themes do not lead to coherent "closed" compositions. The result stands between an all-encompassing composition, a perfectly ordered world of classical architecture and a landscape of "open" free form containing the possibility of disorder.

The slow elaboration of architectural materials inherited from antiquity into a formal canon has several times been linked to the development of a vocabulary, a grammar, and a syntax of architecture. This analogy is particularly tempting when one looks down a classical street where a multitude of town houses in shifting modes and changing rhythms relate to each other in a civilized manner, like persons engaged in a protocolar official manner or in a polite conversational occasion sprinkled with pleasantries. As in a string of words when people are chatting, there is endless "variety," "accident" together with "predictable repetition" and turns of phrases inserted out of courtesy in the midst of an argument or the transmission of information. This wonderful universe is made possible only by some kind of underlying normative apparatus that controls the entrance of elements into the discourse. In architecture, this controlling apparatus is parataxis.

The analogy of architecture to a conversation is appealing, but it can give a reductive and misleading image of the function of classical buildings as vehicles of information and social convention and of the generative rules that allow buildings to "talk" and to "behave" socially. *Decor,* or decorum, as already mentioned, expresses the fit or felicitous relation between genera and deity, nobility, kinship ties, professional affiliation, social position, occasionally ethnic roots, and finally economic standing. In this context an elaborate iconography developed during the Renaissance together with sculptural allegories, emblemata, and devices. These iconographic elements, assembled into larger urban wholes, respond to pragmatic problems, such as the type of message that facades should be relaying. Despite the resulting articulation of classical architecture, we cannot speak of a "grammar" or "syntax" of its figures in the same sense in which these terms are used in language. Such terms confuse rather than explain classical architecture as a cultural social phenomenon. Other categories must be developed. Rhetoric is probably more relevant. It is in Aristotle, Cicero, Quintilian, and Longinus that one must search for the categories that describe the expressive power of classical architecture. One must investigate the figures of eloquent speech. Suggestion, embellishment, metaphor, and analogy are powerful tools of persuasion and ultimately of social control.

At the risk of being accused of being environmental determinists, we would like to suggest that the coherence of parataxis has united people as it has united formal patterns. But the social unity has been limited, more limited than the formal one. Conventions have separated those who have been part of a group or class, confining them into well-defined partitions and positions isolated from those who were not part of this group. To walk down a street complete with classical facades during the eighteenth century meant reading the pattern of social registry of the town or, even more, a discourse legitimizing the structure of status and power of that society. It was a mechanism of social control but a powerless device in arresting the gathering storm by the end of the ancien régime.

The hedonistic response to public places shaped by the formula of parataxis and further elaborated by the figures of eloquence and the rhetoric of influence is not an innate reaction to form but an acquired, socially determined interaction. The passive, mindless consumption of these architectural parades, of the feats of parataxis in street and square compositions, can become a form of conformity.

It is no paradox, therefore, that reactions to these classical public places have varied. There have been times of massive acceptance; there have been moments of violent resistance. The classical parade has appeared both as a universal, rational constitution and as an empty, repressive dogma. There have been periods when classical architecture seemed to open unlimited frontiers, as at the moment of its reception in France during the Renaissance or during the spread of Palladianism in eighteenth-century England. In these moments, the task of the architect was to develop and elaborate a canon whose foundations seemed unshaken although never completely revealed. Witnesses to this act of faith were numerous parataxis patterns formed almost spontaneously across the major cities of these countries. Almost all strata of society felt compelled to carry out what they saw as the fulfillment of the classical architecture program. In the major institutions and in the most humble house and shed, every architectural member was delineated between cap and plinth, every facade terminated by a corona, every placement of a window obeyed a silent prosody. But there have also been periods of massive discontent, of preoccupation with the paradoxes and anomalies of the classical canon—any aspect that would demonstrate what was seen as the oppression. This anticlassicism is among the roots of the regionalist and nationalist movements of the last three centuries, when the calm of parataxis was disrupted and no building could fit compatibly between two others.

172. Facades and plans of town-
houses for persons of every means
(Le Muet 1623).

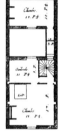

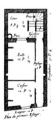

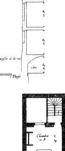

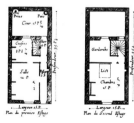

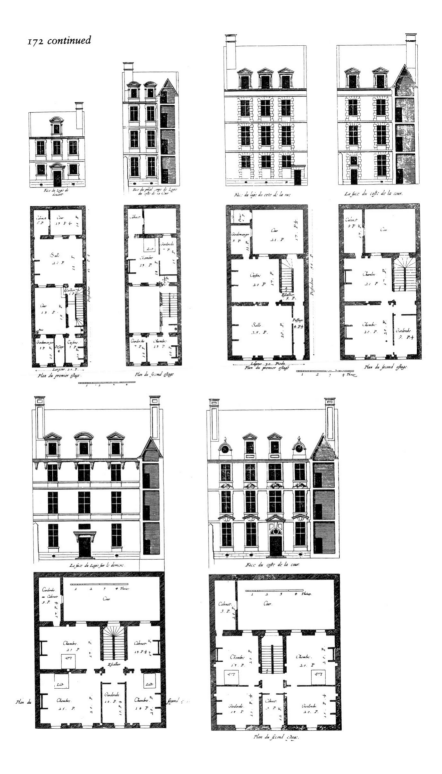

Face du corps de Logis
sur le deuant

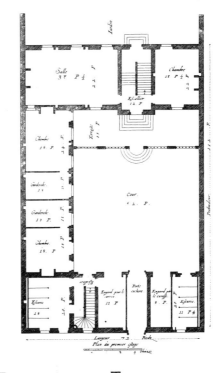

Plan du premier estage

Face du corps de Logis de deuant

La face du Logis de deuant

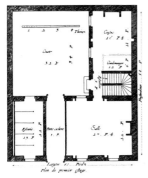

Plan du premier estage

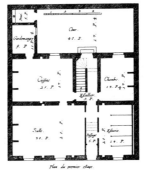

Plan du premier estage

173. Facades of Dutch patrician townhouses (Vingboons 1648–1674).

174. Facades and plans of town-houses. Note changes due to the application of a different genus or to the elaboration of the plan (Neufforge 1757–1780).

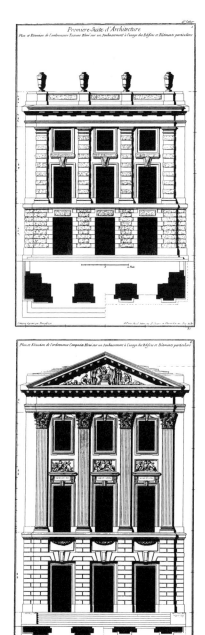

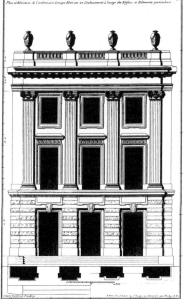

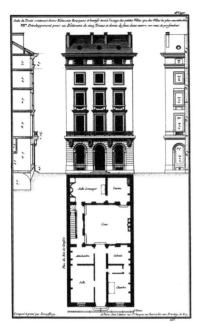

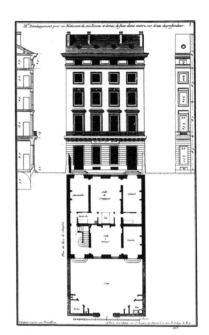

174 continued

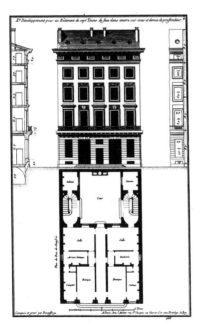

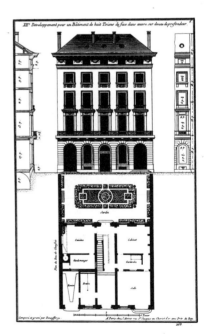

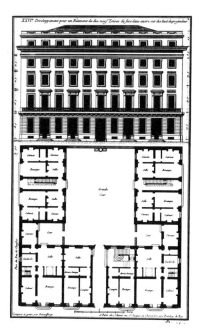

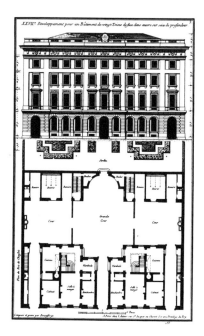

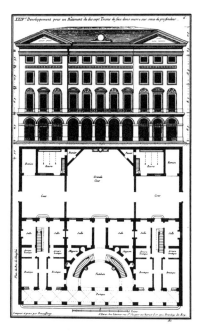

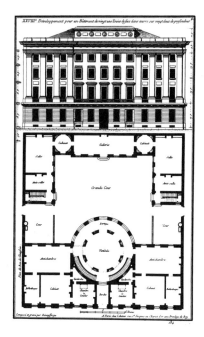

III WHY CLASSICISM?

6 Entaxis: Confrontations and Conflicts

This chapter follows from the previous in a logical rather than chronological way. Parataxis, as we have just seen, is a specific means of responding to the pragmatic social demand felt increasingly from the Renaissance on for the orderly sequence of classical facades in a street or in a square. *Entaxis* is a compositional approach of much greater ambition than parataxis, because it is preoccupied with taxis extending not only in a linear direction but in all directions.

It is a concern that we sense as we move away from the canonical Periclean Golden Age and away from mainland Greece, first eastward to Ionia, then westward toward Rome—a concern for generating a larger taxis schema that will cope not only with the individual building but also with assemblages of buildings as coherent compositions. Hence we have the Hippodamian town plan, a schema infinite in size but limited in possibilities.

The Hippodamian system is attributed to Hippodamos the Miletian of the fifth century B.C., a man greatly interested in political theory and of eccentric appearance. He wore his hair long, not a serious sign in Athens according to Aristotle, who was as doubtful of Hippodamos's political ideas as of his hair length. But thanks to Aristotle we know that Hippodamos "invented the division of cities in blocks" and that he was invited by Pericles to design Peiraeus, or "cut it up" in the words of Aristotle. It is questionable whether Hippodamos single-handedly "invented" this way of planning large assemblages of buildings. He probably codified, systematized, and wrote about ideas that were current in the Ionian world at that time, taking the rectangular grid taxis schema from the individual temple and applying it to whole cities. One can see the Hippodamian system implemented in the plans of Miletos, Priene, and Knidos. Within the repetitive grid sections, most buildings are accommodated but not really rigorously inscribed. There is a tolerance, even a parity, between the circumjacent pattern and the circumscribed one, but never complete integration.

In the sanctuary complexes, taxis divides the space lying between the temple and the surrounding stoas, introducing besides the orthogonal grid the tripartition schema to complexes of buildings. The site of Asclepeion at Cos of the second century is an example. In the first century, in sacred Roman vast compositions, such as the precincts of the Temple of Fortura in Palestrina, Hercules Victor in Tivoli, and even later the Imperial *fora* of Rome, some aspects of genera differentiation and of metric patterning were introduced in addition to tripartition and the grid schema. These other aspects had been lacking in the wight of the Asclepeion and in the Hippodamian cities.

This expanded application of the classical poetics of order occurs increasingly during the period of the Dominate, the imperial period of Rome, a time when, surprisingly, single buildings became less finely structured, conceptually less wrought to perfection, to *teleiotis*. We find the culmination of this development in the Imperial Palace of Diocletian on the Dalmatian coast in Spalato.

All efforts since the Renaissance point to two directions already marked by the Spalato complex:

1. Enlargement of the area of applicability of the whole classical canon to cover large complexes that include several heterogeneous buildings;

2. Creation of genuinely new building types as integral parts of these larger compositional entities—articulation of buildings into the end, middle, or beginning sections of a larger plan.

These efforts led to the palatial complexes, such as Versailles (figure 148) or the Escorial (figure 142), projects we have already seen in our anthology.

But these vast Renaissance and post-Renaissance projects did not provide new compositional patterns and new plan types; on the contrary, they served to push even further the contradictions between classical composition and its surroundings. All the new city planning ideas of the Brunelleschi era for Florence, of the Sixtus V period for Rome, under the ancien régime for Paris simply made the temenos more colossal without reforming or advancing its conceptual framework. In these works, what the poetics of order gained in scale, it lost in rigor.

The apparent disorder of the sites of Periclean and pre-Periclean classical antiquity is a problem that has disturbed many architectural observers since the nineteenth century. Apart from picturesque rationalizations or romantic justifications of sites of antiquity, two interpretations emerged. It was believed either that buildings had been haphazardly placed on a site or that the site had been organized according to a hidden order. Taking for granted the first hypothesis, Schinkel's proposal (1834) for a palace on the top of the Acropolis of Athens desperately sought to cover up the embarrassing unrelatedness of the antique buildings on it. The second speculation led to a number of studies, such as Doxiadis's (1937) (see figure 175). Doxiadis abandoned the obviously untenable paradigm that identified taxis in an ancient Greek site by the use of the schema of a rectangular grid. Instead, he proposed a polar one. Within this schema buildings are viewed from the grid's center at an angle. In this manner one can look at them in a more complete way, testing the coherence of the system. One embraces two sides of the buildings in a single glance rather than their facade only, an idea probably borrowed by Choisy (1899). In Doxiadis's opinion, this polar schema was prior to the Hippodamian system of the fifth century B.C., what we have referred to as the gridiron or rectangular grid schema.

The most intriguing application of the Doxiadis schema was to the Acropolis of Athens (figure 175). Here Doxiadis speculated that within the polar grid the buildings occupied the stressed parts and the surrounding landscape the unstressed ones. Later, Scully (1962) made this notion of participation of the landscape in the composition a key ingredient in his own writing on classical temple sites.

Doxiadis's schema was more ingenious than correct. It revealed the analytical, speculative capabilities of the author rather than the genuine spatial logic of the ancient Greek sites and the classical approach to composition. The author admits in fact "the lack of contemporary reference" to such a system. And written evidence suggests that classical architecture most likely regarded buildings as sealed off from their surroundings.

Often, not only in classical antiquity but also in the Renaissance, vast

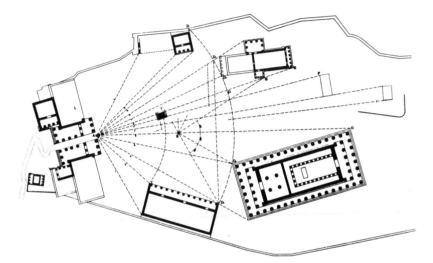

175. Polar grid schema applied to
the Acropolis of Athens (Doxiadis
1937).

accumulations of classical works did not result in larger-scale compositions unless conceived from the very beginning as integral complex
wholes, as in the Palace of Versailles or the palatial projects of Peyre
shown here. Groups of classical buildings tended to constitute assemblages full of formal conflicts and unresolvable compositional ambiguities, spatial fragments and deformations, a disordered mass of
orderly units.

Such sites of petrified confrontations were eventually seen by late
mannerists and early romantics of the eighteenth century as points of
departure of a new formal idiom, a new spatial game, a collage incor-
porating unfinished, cut out, and broken shapes. Such violations of
taxis fascinated designers such as Piranesi who found in them an al-
legorical image (see figure 176) of the impotence, incompleteness, and
cultural decline of the ancien régime. His famous *Antichità Romane*
(1748), setting up the aesthetics of a new, anticlassical order, is a bitter
moral invective.

Besides such formal conflicts between self-contained individual classical works, there were cases of outward clashes between an invading
aggressive classical manner and inherent, existing regional idioms of
design. This was repeatedly the case with a type of urban renewal that
historians have called antiquization.

Antiquization is a term coined by architectural historians to refer to
the Renaissance practice of giving a city the appearance of ancient
Rome or Athens through the introduction of structures organized in the
classical mode. These were occasionally temporary, as in the case of the
"cérémonies à l'antique"—public events of a political content—but
more frequently permanent. This phenomenon became visible in Rome
and Florence and in the other major Italian towns around the fifteenth
century and spread through the cities of the north—Lyon and Paris,
Antwerp and London—throughout all the world, up to our times (Jacquot 1956; Jacquot and Konigson 1971).

As the articulate writings by Pierre Patte (1756, 1769) on Paris indicate, a common way to carry out antiquization is to insert a correcting
taxis schema in a given area of the city, such as a polar grid (see figures
177–179). Often, this grid schema organized space within an existing
urban fabric by inverting the way it organized a building. Instead of an
enclosed world, it created an enclosing one. Old buildings and streets
were mutilated, "aligned" to conform to the new order. Then the gen-

176. Details of a reconstructed
Roman city plan from Piranesi
(1748).

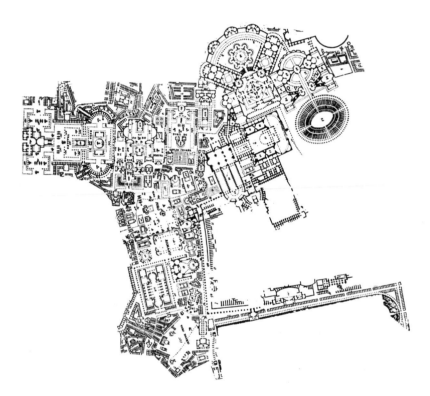

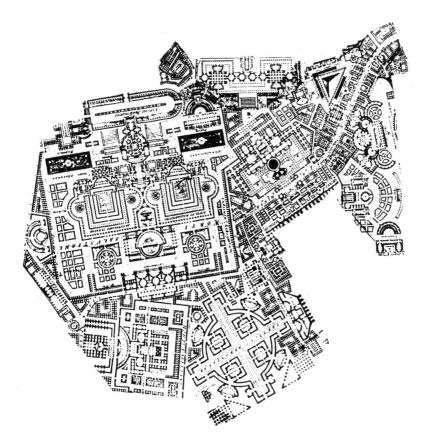

era and symmetry were applied in order to compose a thin slice of a building or even a two-dimensional epidermic wall.

Obviously such insertions and interventions have meant different things at different times and places. They have been the result of an effort to manifest the public face of the city that was taking priority over the private realm. They have been acts of resistance, creations of a collective representation of society against the growing appropriation of space by the individual. Or, finally, they have been acts of policing, desperate efforts of the despotic state to claim legitimacy and to assist the internal colonization of urban territories by economic interests.

The evolving social, economic, political meanings of classicism are complex and lie beyond the scope of this book. Whatever the intentions behind such classicizing undertakings, from the formal point of view they were self-defeating. Cities were cut up, and alien tissue was grafted onto them in the name of formal consistency. Conflicts did not disappear; they just changed locus. Instead of pitting building against building, they set buildings against themselves by forcing them to adapt to an alien order. In the effort to spread classical realm, urban refurbishings lost the most fundamental achievement of the early classical thinking, the temenos, the conception of a contained totality as a world free of contradiction.

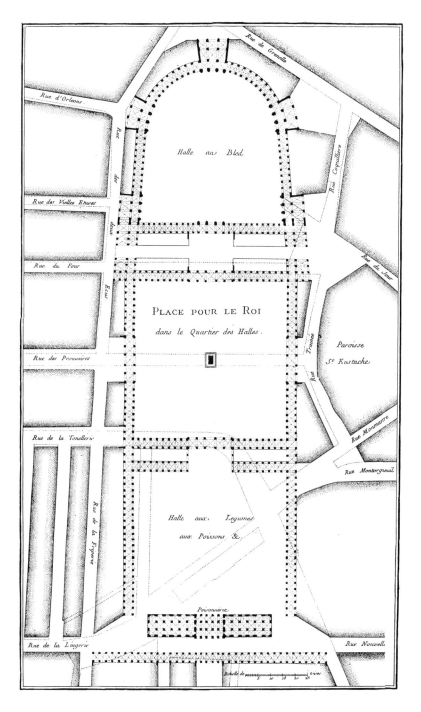

Rue de Grenelle

Rue d'Orleans

Rue Coquilliere

Rue des

deur

Halle au Bled

Rue des Vielles Etuves

Rue du Four

Ecu

Rue du Jour

PLACE POUR LE ROI

dans le Quartier des Halles.

Rue des Prouvaires

Paroisse
St Eustache

Trunée

Rue

Rue de la Tonellerie

Rue Montmartre

Rue Montorgueuil

Rue de la Friperie

Halle aux Legumes
aux Poissons &.

Poissonnerie

Rue de la Lingerie

Rue Nouvelle

Echelle de

177. Patte (1765).

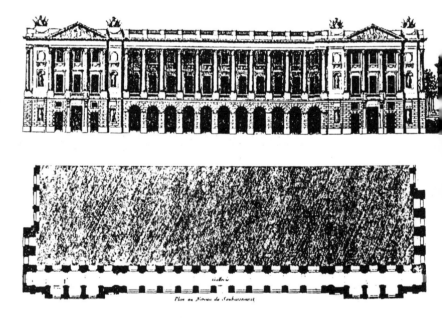

178. Patte (1765).

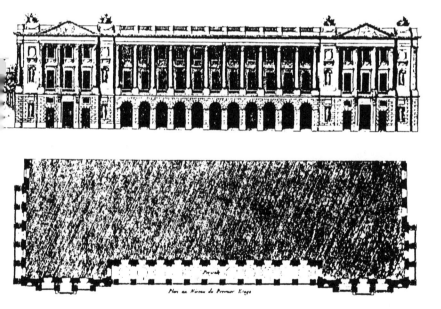

Plan au Niveau du Premier Étage

Pl. LV.

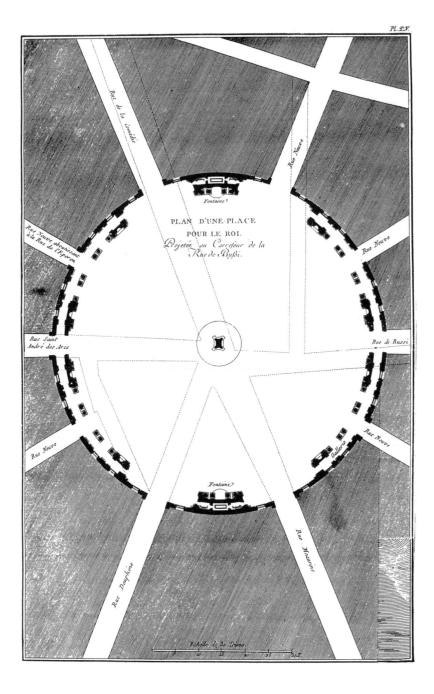

PLAN D'UNE-PLACE
POUR LE ROI.
Projetée au Carrefour de la
Rue de Bussi.

179. Patte (1765).

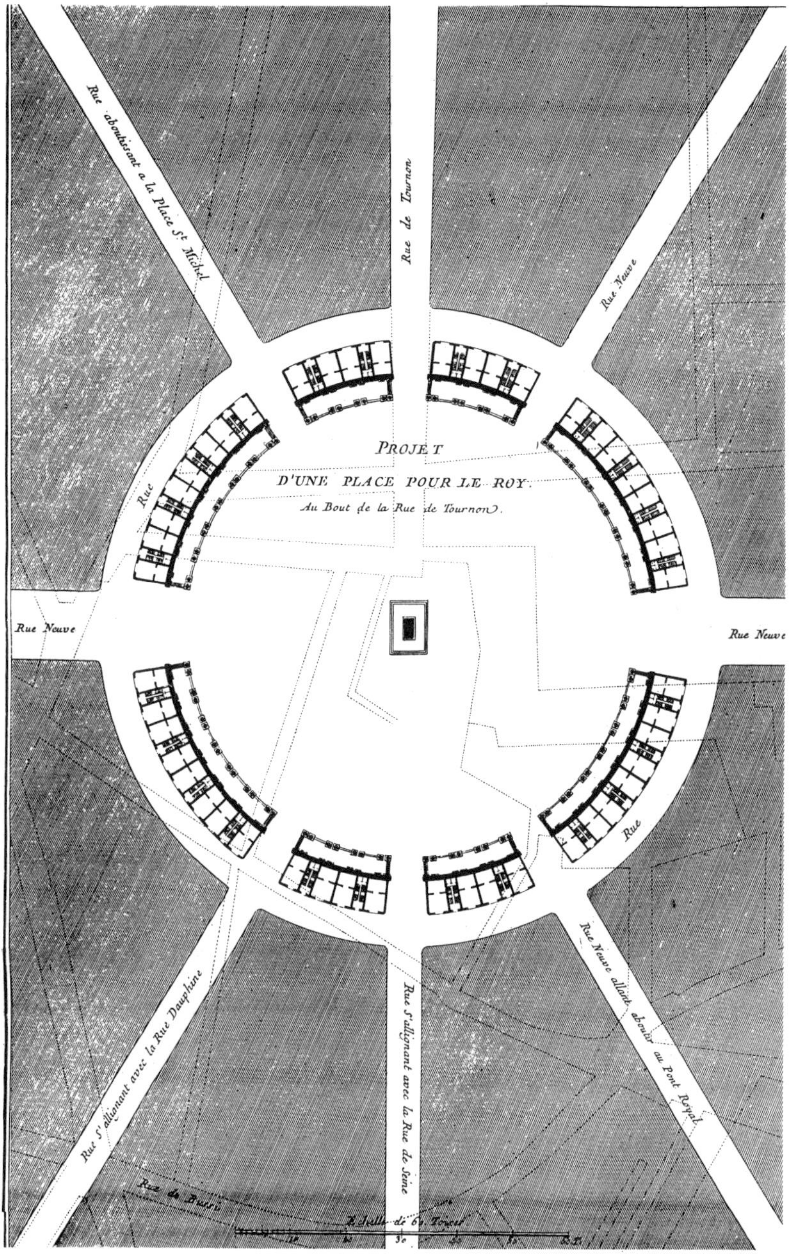
PROJET
D'UNE PLACE POUR LE ROY.
Au Bout de la Rue de Tournon.
Rue de Tournon
Rue aboutissant a la Place St Michel
Rue Neuve
Rue
Rue Neuve
Rue Neuve
Rue
Rue Neuve allant aboutir au Pont Royal
Rue S'alignant avec la Rue de Seine
Rue S'alignant avec la Rue Dauphine
Rue de Bussi

180. Patte (1765).

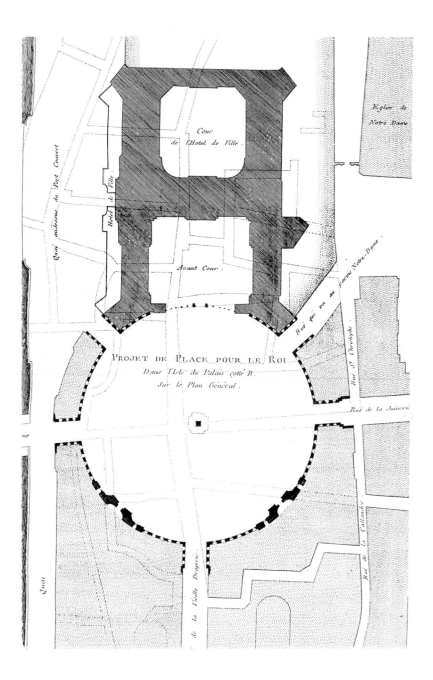

Cour
de l'Hotel de Ville.

Avant Cour.

Hotel de Ville

Quai anciennement du Port Couvert

Eglise de
Notre Dame

Rue qui va au parvis Notre-Dame

Rue St Christophe

PROJET DE PLACE POUR LE ROI
Dans l'Isle du Palais cotté B.
Sur le Plan Général.

Rue de la Juiverie

Rue de la Callendre

Quai

de la Vieille Draperie

181. Patte (1765).

7 Critical Classicism: The Tragic Function

We have seen how painstaking and demanding the poetics of classical order is and some of its potential dangers. An obvious question to ask now is why apply this poetics, why create a perfect world within a world, a temenos? This question carries us even further away from the domain of pure formal analysis of classical architecture than at any other point in this book, toward the territory of meaning and social use. Our intention, on the other hand, is to remain within the realm of poetics in the Aristotelian sense, where poetics is linked to the tragic function. More specifically, we want to find out how a classical building makes us understand reality deeply and how it makes us assume a critical stance in the face of this reality beyond other roles that a building might also play, other meanings and uses it might have outside the tragic meaning and use.

Our first task was to discuss the means of formal composition. Now our task is to investigate the aims, to identify precisely what the tragic meaning and use of a building is.

We have already touched in passing on cases in which the meaning of classical forms has been linked with larger iconographic systems, such as the neoplatonist cosmology or what has been called, rather awkwardly, antiquization. In the case of neoplatonic iconography, churches, palaces, gardens, or whole cities have been given specific forms, which we also encounter in paintings or in prose and poems, that agree with those of the cosmos presumably. In the second case, during ceremonies and celebrations the same type of object has been dressed up *à l'antique* in order to suggest parallels in the mind of the beholder between ancient regimes and contemporary political powers and thus to legitimize the latter by analogy (Jacquot 1956; Jacquot and Konigson 1971). A further study of the use of the classical idiom shows classical architecture to have been engaged in many contradictory meanings and uses since the Renaissance. Classical buildings have been mentioned as part of a movement of antiquization in the Renaissance and as supporters of a militant culture of the same period, legitimizing the new world order of science, the market, industry, and a kind of limited democracy. Up to the end of the eighteenth century, they were used to give support to the ideas of *homo fabricus,* an *exemplum virtutis* of the new way of bourgeois life. But before the republican propagandists of these periods rediscovered the classical column and used it as a prop to create settings to advance the cause of the political assassination of tyrants (as in David's *Brutus* (1789)) or to promote the idea of private sacrifice for public good (as in David's *Socrates* (1787)), the classical column lived happily in the bosom of the private boudoirs of the houses of the old regime.

In this century, Lewis Mumford indisputably demonstrated the explicit social commitment of the Eastern United States financial establishment to the classicized skyscraper. Well known also is the attachment to some kind of classicism by the nazi culture and of the Soviet culture of the Stalinist period. During the same century, in the 1920s, the classical canon, with its apparent detached diachronic impartiality, was employed as an argument for art for art's sake at a moment of major social and economic upheavals that demanded the mobilization of any cultural potential, including architecture, in a campaign of unprecedented social change.

The list of contradictory involvements of classical architecture is too long and too far beyond the scope of this essay to be included. Such shifts in meaning and use are not particular to classical architecture. The ambiguity of architectural form is the rule rather than the exception in architecture.

Classical architecture has also been attached to another iconographic system, that of tectonics, and, through it, to functionalism. This approach to classical architecture has been traditionally associated with a passage in Vitruvius, where he speaks about several carved or sculpted members or ornaments of the genera and interprets them as originating in the details of older wood construction (*De Architectura*, bk. IV, chap. II, para. 5). The genera are *veris naturae deducta*, deduced from true nature. The building imitates reality as its final validation; "what cannot occur in reality" cannot be treated in imitation correctly. Since Vitruvius's time, various details of the classical temple—the dentils and the mutules, the triglyphs and the guttae, the abacus and the echinus— have often been described as geometrized, ordered "abstraction" or "generalization" of the construction elements of the older wooden temples. Similarly, plan typological components, such as porticoes, stoas, and atria, have been seen as "abstractions" and "generalizations" of older wooden construction types and ultimately of the "archetypal" primitive hut, now petrified and canonized.

In functionalism, we have an iconographic system that reduces the complexity and universality of classical architecture to a statement in stone about wooden buildings or about tectonics, the properties of strength of materials, the behavior of forces, or any of the other aspects of construction. This is not to say that classical architecture is cut out from reality or even from the reality of construction. Just the contrary. It is all tangled up with reality. But this relation conveys much more information than the technological, historical reality of constructions hoisted in remote times on the banks and hills of legendary cities and groves scattered all over the Middle East, northern Africa, and the southern Mediterranean coast, or of any other constructions.

A classical building, when seen as a temenos, as a world within the world, factured by the rule-based actions of its architect, is a representation of different phenomena of reality.

Taxis, the genera, symmetry, and their numerous schemata set up representations of relations in an "analoglike" manner whose chains, matrices, lattices, and even more complex patterns of reasoning are implicit in the formal patterning of the work. Thus, although the formal patterns of classical buildings might depict specific historical events or aspects of construction, they are also capable of embodying abstract relations of quantity and space, out of which one can infer, again analogically, statements about many facets of reality: the reality of nature, the reality of thinking, the reality of human association, and the reality of future artifacts.

In this sense, good classical architectural compositions are ingenious essays in stone, intelligently argued dialectics and hermeneutics. This is true of most ancient Greek temples and most buildings, for example, by Alberti or Palladio. In these buildings partitioning, ornament, and rhythm, in the sense we have been using here, form a conceptual structure for implementing a major part of the program of classical architecture: to create representations of reality; to explore through the formal relations of the building the architecture of reality; to identify in reality independence, equivalence, subalternation, contrarity, symmetry, transitivity, correlation, identity, whole, continuity; to study how space works, how we can work in space, how our mind works, and how we can work together as a society.

But the formal patterns of a classical building can also relate to reality in a diametrically different, nonmimetic way. We call this relation *foregrounding* and *strangemaking*. The world of the building in this case is not only about what is but also about what must be done, not only about truth and epistemology but also about goodness and morality.

Foregrounding in architecture comes from the theories of the literary poetics formulated by the Prague School of linguistics of the 1930s and in particular by Jan Mukařovský, and by the Russian Formalists of the 1920s, especially Victor Shklovsky. According to this theory, the essential feature of a literary text is the transformation of ordinary language into poetic language. "Foregrounding" as translated by Garvin (1964, p. 9) (in the original Czech *aktualisace*), or what Shklovsky called "roughened form," brings about certain characteristics of a text that make its linguistic organization—phonetic, grammatical, syntactic, semantic—deviate from ordinary use. Thus the *poetic* identity of a building depends not on its stability, on its function, or on the efficiency of the means of its production but on the way in which all the above have been limited, bent, and subordinated by purely formal requirements. What distinguishes a classical building as a poetic object from ordinary buildings is there, on the surface, in its formal organization. But beyond this formal veil lies the act of foregrounding through which selected aspects from the reality of a building are recast into formal patterns. The resulting quality of *architecturalness* is not a portrait of reality. It is its critical reconstruction.

The relation between the formal and the social needs of a work of art are often taken in a mechanistic way. As an example of this, Shklovsky refers to Herbert Spencer's (1882) comments on rhythm in poetry.

Spencer compared the "varying concussions" of the body, which, if they recur "in definite order," permit the body to adjust better to the "unarranged articulations" the mind receives, which "rhythmically arranged" may permit it to "economize its energies by anticipating the attention required for each syllable." Here, rhythm is a means of overcoming "friction and inertia" that "deduct from . . . efficiency." Shklovsky (1965, p. 24) criticizes this simple-minded economicist interpretation of rhythm, which he calls the "groaning together" of the "members of the work crew." To this naive approach he juxtaposes a theory of form taken from Tolstoy, where poetry has a much more complex social function, one that acknowledges the presence of conflict in society, the need for social criticism, and the social engagement of poetry as a critical activity. This function of poetry, as of all art, is to counteract the destructive impact of everyday social life, of the established social relations. It is to arrest and cleanse that which, in the words of Tolstoy, "devours works, clothes, furniture, one's wife, and the fear of war": the deadening effect of routine and its implacable, almost algebraic predictability. Shklovsky (1965) refers to the entry of March 1, 1897, from Tolstoy's diaries. It is worth repeating part of it here.

I was cleaning a room and, meandering about, approached the divan and couldn't remember whether or not I had dusted it. Since these movements are habitual and unconscious, I could not remember and felt that it was impossible to remember. . . . If some conscious person had been watching, then the fact could be established. If, however, no one was looking, or looking unconsciously, if the whole complex lives of many people go on unconsciously, then such lives are as if they had never been. (p. 12)

Tolstoy's way of "pricking the conscience," according to Shklovsky, is to "strangemake" (our translation of the original Russian *ostraneniye*), to make people aware of the condition of their lives by making a world in which familiar things are reset in a slightly different order. Aristotle, in his *Poetics,* had already remarked that "by deviating in exceptional cases from the *normal* idiom, the language will gain distinction" (ch. XXII, para. 4). He had even used the notion of "strange" (*xenikon*) (ch. XXII, para. 1) for words that had been rendered phonetically, grammatically, syntactically, or semantically deviant. In his *Art of Rhetoric* the notion of "strange" (distant, remote) is linked with "removing from ordinary" and with august dignity of poetic discourse (bk. III, ch. II, para. 2, 3). The foregrounding of certain aspects of a building that one observes in classical architecture can be seen as such necessary deviations from the "normal idiom" to achieve distancing from established social perceptions and practices. Brecht's theory of "estrangement" (in the original German *Verfremdung*) in drama comes to remarkably similar conclusions. "Worldmaking," if we may return for an instant to our first chapter where we referred to Goodman's term, is in this sense strangemaking.

Taxis, genera, shape, metric patterns, and figures in classical architecture make doors, windows, walls, parapets, ceilings, and floors depart from their normal everyday range of habit dictated by ordinary uses, such as supporting, bracing, pulling, insulating, jointing, storing, and surveying. As a hero of a tragedy is an ordinary person "typified" as the result of strangemaking, so the temenos is a "typified" defamiliarized ordinary habitat, hence the presence of construction details in heroizing patterns of the classical idiom. And as a tragedy imitates reality, makes strange, and formalizes a special action in order to inspire "fear or pity" (*Poetics,* ch. IX, para. 11), so a classical building in its very architecturalness makes strange a real ordinary construction. Hence the architectural methods of poetic deflection alter the location, position, dimension, configuration, and number of architectural elements.

In classical architecture the new arrangements and the new compositional wholes that emerge create a poetic world next to the ordinary one. "Catharsis," or cleansing, is the word Aristotle uses to describe this process in a tragedy. The effect of this juxtaposition of the two realms, poetic and ordinary, is purification, which in the modern world has a clear critical purpose as the divinatory one had in archaic culture. The building, as a *temenos,* can be seen as bringing about the same kind of catharsis a tragedy does. It takes the existing reality and reorganizes it through strangemaking on a higher cognitive level. It·provides a new frame in which to understand reality, with which to "cleanse" away an obsolete one. The means are formal, the effect is cognitive, the purpose moral and social.

In a building as in a tragedy, it is difficult to disentangle how much the use of the classical canon leads to strangemaking and how much leads to imitation, to, one is tempted to say, "samemaking," how much through formalization the building confronts reality and how much it represents it. It is equally difficult to specify the degree to which formalization, generalization, and strangemaking separate the work from the world without concurrently engaging it critically with reality. It all depends on how the work is being used, on our intentions as much as on the structure of the work itself.

It is even more difficult to ascertain the interpretations that classical formal patterns might have when applied in ways outside the canon. Let us take a chance and venture, although this is rightly the topic of a new study, that there are three major applications of partial use of the classical canon: (1) "Citationism" of classical motifs, or so-called free-wheeling classicism; (2) syncretism; and (3) the use of classical frag-ments in architectural "metastatement."

Under citationism belongs the "classicism" of kitsch, of consumer products, of propaganda, and of even more ambitious cultural objects, "prestige" buildings and in several occasions *some* of the so-called post-modernist buildings. The method applied appears as a libertarian quo-tation of classical pieces, especially motifs within an alien body. This is the logic of deception, through the piecemeal reuse of classical compo-nents, that of "associationism," of "reductionism," which sets up the building as a simulacra of reality, an "as if" "scenographic" reality in the place of the foregrounded reality of critical worldmaking. Strangemaking is replaced by *overfamiliarization* and fake intimacy. The temple is not set apart from the world; it lies there accessible and up for grabs. With this vanishes the imitative heroic character, the representational tragic, poetic function of classical architecture and, together with it, the critical stance. The temenos is used as an imprison-ing and deadening agent, and the canon is turned into a large laboratory for manufacturing false consciousness. This vulgarization of the work does not in the least make it more public. The only potential of illusion-ism is private indulgence.

When the meaning of the temenos has been banalized or polluted, critical intent has had to search for alternative ways of expression out-side the classical canon. Strangemaking has then had to take a path that is altogether different: to destroy the classical canon, now itself the embodiment of "the deadening effect of habitualization." A new pas-sage has had to be opened up—disrupting symmetries, shifting axes, breaking corners, bursting through boundaries, abandoning hierarchi-zation and tripartition, opting instead for deformed and irregualr pat-terns, ignoring elements, members, and their ranks. Catharsis has had to flee the classical schemata of taxis, genera, and symmetry and forge another formal anticlassical canon.

This has happened several times in the past, and it can occur again. Such was the case with the genesis of the picturesque in the eighteenth century and, in our own, with constructivism, modernism, and De Stijl. In the works of El Lissitsky and Iakov Chernikov (figure 183), of Mendelsohn and Luckhardt, of Gerrit Rietveld and Theo van Doesburg (figure 182), new kinds of *temene* were set up. They were no less radical than Arnold Schönberg's twelve tone method and Anton von Webern's serial music. These architectural projects might have been awkward and formidable in the eyes of classicist conformists. But was classicism itself not awkward and formidable in most eyes at the dawn of the Renaissance?

Let us return to the two other partial applications of the classical canon: syncretism and metastatement. Unlike citationism, they do not cause nostalgia or illusion. They can be pessimistic or ironic, polemical or adversarial, but always critical. In the case of syncretism more than one canon is used simultaneously in the same design, even if these are at odds and produce non sequitur effects. In the second case, that of metastatement, a world of higher visual statements is built that refers to the classical canon. Classical segments are used as means of saying something about classicism, they become, in other words, statements within a higher-level metastatement.

In both cases—syncretism and metastatement—fragments of the classical canon are used as means of questioning a dogmatic or quasi-automatic, routine application of the classical order.

Examples of the combination of syncretism and metastatement are to be found in early Renaissance works, in Brunelleschi or Alberti, or in late Renaissance works. More recently they can be found in the "neoclassical modernist" buildings, which recall, in their formal organization and in their "syncretist" or "metastatement" approach, parallel efforts of Stravinsky, Picasso, André Gide, and Ezra Pound. Among these let us single out Le Corbusier's Villa Savoye (1928–1929) and the buildings of Chandigarh, which apply certain aspects of classical taxis and symmetry while violating others and ignoring altogether the genera. The same can be said about Mies van der Rohe's Crown Hall (figure 188), Commonwealth Apartments (figures 184, 187), and Seagram Building (figure 186), where there is a constant shift from the classical to the De Stijl canon. Finally a similar observation can be made for the most intriguing plan of Aldo van Eijck's orphanage at Ijsbaanpad near Amsterdam (figure 190), and some buildings of the Italian rationalists of the 1930s, especially the work of Giuseppe Terragni, where the two canons, classical and modernist, are joined in a perfect formal amalgam.

The difference between the three uses of segments of the classical canon—citation or overfamiliarizing, syncretism, and metastatement—is fundamental; it is not one of degree, but of essence. These approaches vary, as we have seen, in how they select and apply pieces of the canon, but they also vary in what they achieve through these selective applications. Clearly in order to disentangle the historically bound differences between "pseudoclassical," "anticlassical," "postclassical," "preclassical," or "metaclassical" projects, we would like to emphasize once more that a separate and detailed study must be undertaken.

In the present interpretation of classical architecture, foregrounding and strangemaking have been stressed ideas that have traditionally been applied to modernism. The rigor and the potential of the critical function of taxis, genera, and symmetry has been pointed out. The purpose has been to recover classical architecture from citationism in the service of the fading Elysium of nostalgia; to elevate it above the status of a funeral, albeit a first class funeral; and to disassociate it from bankrupt, seedy lawyers' waiting rooms, from sleepy hotel receptions, from forgotten locked storage rooms in the late autumnal afternoons of declining Mediterranean ports, from gardens cluttered with decapitated columns, lame arches, stairs leading to collapsed platforms, door frames complete with entablatures standing in the void and blocked with debris.

The world of classical architecture today is a world of scattered forms that in their incompleteness can be seen as icons of decomposition. But they can also be seen as unfinished pictures of a promised world, like the suspended golden hour in the landscapes of Claude Lorrain to be taken as part of the nightfall or of the dawn. The time direction of the classical fragments that still surround us points to two diametrically opposed paths. We have taken the one leading away from the joyful pessimism of that grand hotel, Abyss.

The critical potentials of classicism might arise from the fact that we belong to a generation of crisis, and frequently, of counterfeit culture, in which there is a disintegration of human relations at every level of association and in which the threat of total war, of total annihilation, is

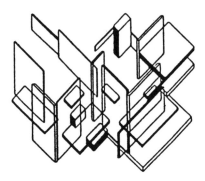

182. Doesburg and van Eesteren
(1925).

183. Chernikov (1933).

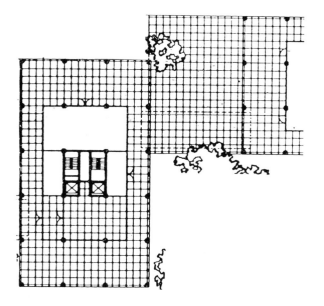

184. De Stijl relation between
buildings, Lakeshore Apartments
(Ludwig Mies van der Rohe).

185. Classical relation between
buildings (Perrault 1673).

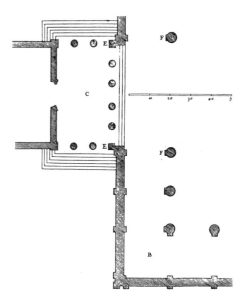

186. Seagram building (L. Mies van der Rohe). Building termination by accentuation.

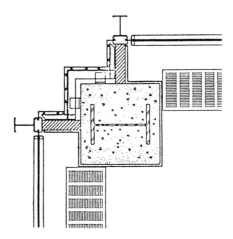

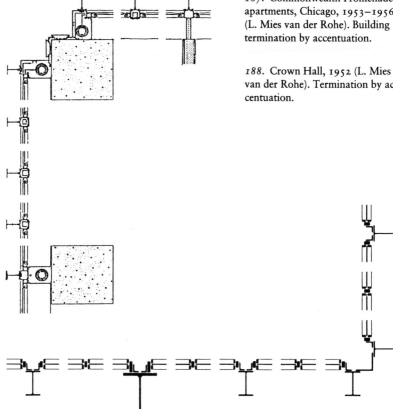

187. Commonwealth Promenade apartments, Chicago, 1953–1956, (L. Mies van der Rohe). Building termination by accentuation.

188. Crown Hall, 1952 (L. Mies van der Rohe). Termination by accentuation.

189. Palais du Luxembourg. Termination by accentuation (Blondel 1752–1756).

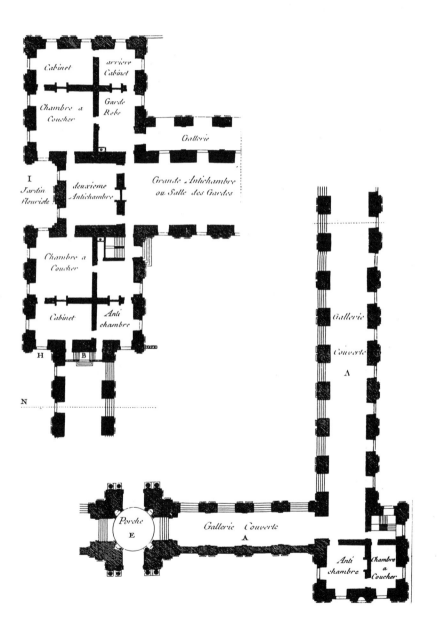

190. Children's Home, Amsterdam, 1958 (Eyck).

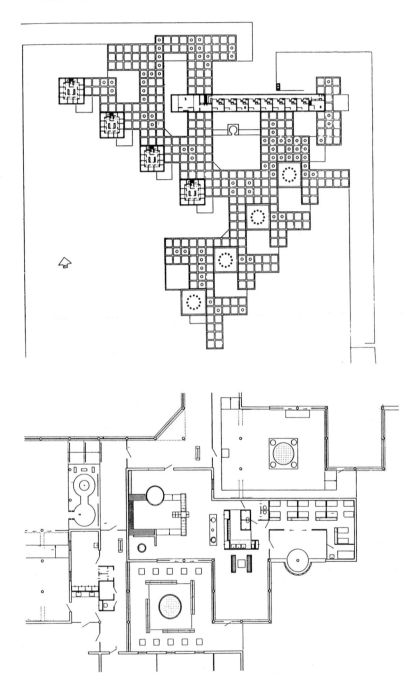

real. Children of happier times might find, in the obsessive efforts of classicism to align, partition, measure, relate, and finish, a discipline of the mind. They might discover in these countless redefinitions of the game of interspacing and termination, superimposition and repetition, an imperative to generate a work free of contradiction. Perhaps they will recognize in classicism a thinking that struggles for consistency and completeness. They might see in this imperative for order and rationality a quest in the domain of thinking—but also what Thomas Mann (1957) called "the highly cherished idea of a perfected humanity."

References

Ackerman, J. S. 1963. "Sources of the Renaissance villa," in *Acts of the Twentieth International Congress of the History of Art*. Princeton, N.J.: Princeton University Press.

Ackerman, J. S. 1967. *Palladio*. Harmondsworth. Revised edition, Penguin, 1977.

Ackerman, J. S. 1983. "The Tuscan/Rustic order: A study in the metaphorical language of architecture," *Journal of the Society of Architectural Historians* 42 (March), pp. 15–34.

Adams, R., and Adams, J. 1773–1778. *The Works in Architecture*. London.

Aristotle. 1975 [c. 330 B.C.]. *Art of Rhetoric*. Cambridge, Mass., and London: Harvard University Press and Heinemann.

Aristotle. 1975 [c. 340 B.C.]. *The Poetics*. Cambridge, Mass., and London: Harvard University Press and Heinemann.

Barozzi, J. (Il Vignola). 1562–1563. *Regola delli cinque Ordini d'Architettura*. Venice.

Berwick, R. C. 1985. *The Acquisition of Syntactic Knowledge*. Cambridge, Mass.: The MIT Press.

Blunt, A. 1970. *Art and Architecture in France, 1500–1700*, English edition. Harmondsworth: Penguin.

Carpenter, R. 1959. *The Esthetic Basis of Greek Art*. Bloomington, Ind.: Indiana University Press.

Carpenter, R. 1970. *The Architects of the Parthenon*. Harmondsworth: Penguin.

Cesariano, C. 1521. *De Architectura*. Como.

Choisy, A. 1899. *Histoire de l'architecture*. Paris.

Cicero. 1948 [55 B.C.]. *De Oratore.* Cambridge, Mass.: Harvard University Press.

Cicero. 1949 [84 B.C.]. *De Inventione.* Cambridge, Mass.: Harvard University Press.

Cicero (?). 1954 [c. 80 B.C.]. *Ad Herennium.* Cambridge, Mass.: Harvard University Press.

Collins, P. 1965. *Changing Ideals in Modern Architecture.* London: Faber.

Colonna, F. 1499. *Hypnerotomachia Poliphili.* Venice.

Cottart, P. 1671. *Recueil des oeuvres.* Paris.

Coulton, J. J. 1977. *Greek Architects at Work.* London: Beekman.

Cousin, J. 1560. *Livre de perspective.* Paris.

d'Aviler, C.-A. 1691. *Cours d'architecture.* Paris.

de Chambray, F. 1659. *Parallèle de l'architecture antique et de la moderne.* Paris.

de Chamoust, R. 1776. *l'Ordre français trouvé dans la nature.* Paris.

Delorme (de l'Orme), P. 1567. *Architecture.* Paris.

Desgodetz, A. 1682. *Edifices antiques de Rome.* Paris.

Doxiadis, C. 1972. *Architectural Space in Ancient Greece.* Cambridge, Mass.: The MIT Press. Original in German, Berlin, 1937.

Durand, J. N. L. 1802–1805. *Précis des leçons d'architecture données à l'Ecole Polytechnique.* Paris: Durand.

Durm, J. 1892. *Die Baukunst der Griechen* (2nd ed.). Leipzig: Kröner.

Durm, J. 1905. *Die Baukunst der Römer* (2nd ed.). Stuttgart.

Egbert, D. D. 1980. *The Beaux-Arts Tradition in French Architecture.* Princeton, N.J.: Princeton University Press.

Eliot, T. S. 1953. "Tradition and the individual talent," in *Selected Prose.* Harmondsworth: Penguin.

Emlyn, H. 1797. *Proposition of a New Order in Architecture.* London.

Epstein, E. L. 1978. *Language and Style.* London: Methuen.

Erlich, V. 1981. *Russian Formalism.* New Haven, Conn.: Yale University Press.

Focillon, H. 1948. *The Life of Forms in Art.* New York: Wittenborn.

Fontanier, P. 1977 [1818]. *Les figures du discours.* Paris: Flammarion.

Forssman, E. 1961. *Dorisch, Ionisch, Korintisch.* Stockholm: Almquist and Wiksell.

Fowler, R. 1966. *Essays on Style and Language.* New York: Humanities Press.

Frankl, P. 1936. *Das System der Kunstwissenschaft.* Brunn/Leipzig.

Frankl, P. 1968. *Principles of Architectural History: The Four Phases of Architectural Style 1420–1900,* James F. O'Gorman, translator. Cambridge, Mass.: The MIT Press. Originally published in 1914 in German.

Freeman, D. C. (ed.). 1981. *Essays in Modern Stylistics.* London: Methuen.

Garvin, P. L. 1964. *A Prague School Reader.* Washington, D.C.: Georgetown University Press.

Giedion, S. 1922. *Spätbarocker und romantischer Klassizismus.* Munich.

Goodman, N. 1981. *Ways of Worldmaking.* Indianapolis, Ind.: Hackett.

Goodyear, W. H. 1912. *Greek Refinements.* New Haven, Conn., and London: Yale University Press.

Grassi, E. 1980. *Die Theorie des Schönen in der Antike.* Köln: Dumont.

Greenhalgh, M. 1978. *The Classical Tradition in Art.* New York: Harper & Row.

Halle, M., and Keyser, S. J. 1981. "Iambic pentameter," in *Essays in Modern Stylistics,* D. C. Freeman (ed.). London: Methuen.

Hamlin, T. F. 1944. *Greek Revival Architecture in America.* New York: Dover.

Hautecoeur, L. 1952–1953. *Histoire de l'architecture classique en France.* Paris: French and European Publications. Originally published in 1943.

Hederer, O. 1976. *Klassizismus.* Müchen: Heyne.

Herrmann, W. 1973. *Claude Perrault.* London: Schwemmer.

Hildebrand, A. 1903. *Das Problem der Form in der Bildenden Kunst.* Strassburg: Haetz.

Honour, H. 1968. *Neo-Classicism.* Harmondsworth: Penguin.

Jacquot, J. 1956. *Les fêtes de la renaissance.* Paris: CNRS. 2 volumes.

Jacquot, J., and Konigson, E. 1971. *Les fêtes de la renaissance.* Paris: CNRS.

Jakobson, R. 1968. "Poetry of grammar and grammar of poetry," *Lingua* 21:597–609.

Jakobson, R. 1973. "The dominant," in *Readings in Russian Poetics,* L. Matejka and K. Pomorska (eds.). Cambridge, Mass.: The MIT Press. Originally published in Russian in 1935.

Jakobson, R., Fant, C. G. M., and Halle, M. 1952. *Preliminaries to Speech Analysis*. Cambridge, Mass.: The MIT Press.

Kohte, J. 1915. *Die Baukunst des Klassichen Altertums*. Braunschweig: von Friedrich.

Krafft, J. C., and Ransonnette, N. 1801–1802. *Plans, coupes et élévations des plus belles maisons et des hôtels à Paris*. Paris.

Kubler, G. 1962. *The Shape of Time*. New Haven, Conn.: Yale University Press.

le Clerc, S. 1714. *Traité d'architecture*. Paris.

Leech, G. N. 1969. *A Linguistic Guide to English Poetry*. London: Longman.

Lemon, L. T., and Reis, M. J. 1965. *Russian Formalist Criticism*. Lincoln, Neb.: University of Nebraska Press.

Lerdahl, F., and Jackendoff, R. 1983. *A Generative Theory of Tonal Music*. Cambridge, Mass.: The MIT Press.

Le Roy, J. D. 1758. *Ruines des plus beaux monuments de la Grèce*. Paris.

Lessing, G. E. 1984. [1776]. *Laocoon*. Baltimore, Md.: Johns Hopkins University Press.

Le VirLoys, R. 1770. *Dictionnaire d'Architecture*. Paris.

Lévi-Strauss, C. 1966. *The Savage Mind*. Chicago, Ill.: University of Chicago Press. Originally published in French in 1962.

MacDonald, W. L. 1965. *The Architecture of the Roman Empire*. New Haven, Conn.: Yale University Press.

Mann, T. 1957. "Goethe and Tolstoy," in *Essays*. New York: Vintage. Originally published in German in 1922.

Marr, D. 1982. *Vision*. San Francisco, Calif.: Freeman.

de Momigny, J. J. 1806. *Cours complet d'harmonie et de composition*. Paris.

Mukarovski, J. 1964. "Standard language and poetic language, in *A Prague School Reader on Esthetics, Literary Structure and Style*, Paul L. Garvin (ed.). Washington, D.C.: Georgetown University Press.

Mumford, L. 1955. *Sticks and Stones*. New York: Dover. Originally published in 1924.

Pain, W. 1786. *British Palladio*. London.

Palladio, A. 1570. *I Quattro Libri dell'Architettura*. Venice.

Panofsky, E. 1939. Introduction to *Studies in Iconology: Humanistic Themes in the Art of the Renaissance.* Oxford: Oxford University Press. Published in 1972 by Harper & Row.

Papert, S. 1967 "Structures et catégories," in *Logique et connaissance scientifique,* J. Piaget (ed.). Paris: French and European Publications.

Patte, P. 1765. *Monuments érigés à la gloire de Louis XV.* Paris.

Patte, P. 1769. *Mémoire sur les objets les plus importants de l'architecture.* Paris.

Percier, C., and Fontaine, P. F. L. 1801. *Palais, maisons et autres édifices modernes.* Paris.

Perrault, C. 1673. *Les dix livres d'architecture.* Paris: Coignard.

Perrault, C. 1683. *Ordonnance des cinq espèces de colonne.* Paris.

Piranesi, G. 1756. *Le Antichità Romane.*

Praz, M. 1969. *On Classicism.* London: Thames and Hudson.

Preminger, A. (ed.). 1965. *Princeton Encyclopedia of Poetry and Poetics.* Princeton, N.J.: Princeton University Press.

Quintilian. 1970 [c. A.D. 95]. *Institutio Oratoria.* Oxford, England: Oxford University Press.

Ratner, L. G. 1980. *Classic Music: Expression, Form, and Style.* New York: Schirmer Books.

Richardson, A. E. 1982. *Monumental Classic Architecture in Great Britain and Ireland.* New York: Norton. Originally published in 1914.

Riemann, H. 1903. *System der musikalischen Rhythmik und Metrik.* Leipzig.

Riepel, J. 1755. *Grundregeln zur Tonordnung insgemein.* Frankfurt and Leipzig.

Robertson, D. S. 1971. *Greek and Roman Architecture.* Cambridge, England: Cambridge University Press. Originally published in 1929.

Rosen, C. 1971. *The Classical Style.* New York and London: Norton. Originally published in French in 1967.

Schinkel, K. F. 1834. Project for a Royal Palace for the Acropolis (pen, black ink, watercolor, white whitening). Inv. no. Schinkel Slg 35b/44. Schinkel Museum, Berlin.

Schopenhauer, A. 1966. *The World as Will and Representation.* New York: Dover.

Scully, V. 1962. *The Earth, the Temple, and the Gods.* New Haven, Conn.: Yale University Press.

Serlio, S. 1619. *Tutte l'opere*. Venice: de Franceschi. Five books originally published in 1537, 1540, 1545, 1547, and 1575.

Shklovsky, V. 1965. "Art as technique," in *Russian Formalist Criticism*, L. T. Lemon and M. J. Reis (eds.). Lincoln, Neb.: University of Nebraska Press.

Shoe, L. 1952. *Profiles of Western Greek Mouldings*. Rome.

Spencer, H. 1882. *The Philosophy of Style*. New York: Humboldt.

Stiny, G. 1980. "Introduction to shape and shape grammars," *Environment and Planning*, sec. B, 7:5–18.

Stuart, J., and Revett, N. 1762. *Antiquities of Athens*.

Tatarkiewicz, W. 1970. *History of Aesthetics I: Ancient Aesthetics*. The Hague and Warsaw: Mouton and PWN.

Thiersch, A. 1889. "Die Proportionen in der Architektur," in *Handbuch der Architektur*, bk. VI, ch. I. Berlin.

Turner, G. W. 1973. *Stylistics*. Harmondsworth: Penguin.

Tzonis, A. 1972. *Towards a Non-Oppressive Environment*. Cambridge, Mass.: The MIT Press.

Tzonis, A., and Lefaivre, L. 1978. *History of Architecture as a Social Science*. Cambridge, Mass.: Harvard Graduate School of Design, Publication Series in Architecture.

Tzonis, A., and Lefaivre, L. 1984. "The question of autonomy in architecture," *The Harvard Architectural Review* 3:25–42.

Valéry, P. 1921. "Eupalinos," in *Architectures*. Paris.

Villalpando, J. B., and Prado, J. 1596–1604. In *Ezechielem Explanationes*. Rome.

Vitruvius. 1931 [before 27 B.C.]. De Architectura. Cambridge, Mass.: Harvard University Press.

Winckelmann, J. J. 1764. *Geschichte der Kunst des Alterthums*. Dresden.

Wittgenstein, L. 1967. *Wittgenstein: Lectures and Conversations on Aesthetics, Psychology and Religious Belief*, Cyril Barrett (ed.). Berkeley, Calif.: University of California Press.

Wittkower, R. 1949. *Architectural Principles in the Age of Humanism*. London: Warburg. Published in 1971 by Norton.

Wittkower, R. 1974. "The Renaissance baluster and Palladio," in *Palladio and English Palladianism*. London: Thames and Hudson.

Wölfflin, H. 1967 [1888]. *Renaissance and Baroque*. Ithaca, N.Y.: Cornell University Press.

Wölfflin, H. 1968. *Classic Art* (3rd ed.). London: Phaidon. Originally published in German in 1899.

Wölfflin, H. 1932. *Principles of Art History.* New York: Dover, Originally published in German in 1915.

Zeitler, R. 1954. *Klassizismus und Utopia.* Stockholm.

Illustration Sources

Alberti, L. B., C. Bartoli, and J. Leoni, *Ten Books on Architecture*. London 1726.

Barbaro, D., *I Dieci Libri . . . di Vitruvio*. Venice 1567. First published in Latin in 1556.

Bertotti-Scamozzi, O., *Le fabbriche e i disegni di Andrea Palladio*. Venice 1796.

Blondel, J. F., *L'architecture française*. Paris 1752–1756.

Briseux, C. E., *Traité du beau essentiel dans les arts appliqué particulière-ment à l'architecture*. Paris 1752.

Campen, J. van, *Afbeelding van 't Stadt Huys van Amsterdam*. Amsterdam 1661.

Cataneo, Senese P., *I quattro primi libri di architettura*. 1554.

Cesariano, C. di Lorenzo, *De architectura*. Como 1521.

Chambers, W., *A Treatise on the Decorative Part of Civil Architecture*. London 1791.

Chernikov, I., *Architectural Fantasy*. 1933.

Colonna, F., *Le Songe de Poliphile*. Paris 1546. First published in Latin, Venice 1449.

Cousin, J., *Livre de perspective*. Paris 1560.

Delorme, P., *L'architecture*. Rouen 1648. First published in 1561 and 1567.

Desgodetz, A., *Les édifices antiques de Rome*. Paris 1682.

Doesburg, Th. van, and C. van Eesteren, *L'architecture vivante*. 1925.

Doxiadis, C., *Raumordnung im griechischen Städtebau*. Berlin 1937. English translation, *Architectural Space in Ancient Greece*, The MIT Press, Cambridge, Massachusetts, 1972.

Du Cerceau, J. A., *Livre d'architecture*. Paris 1559.

Du Cerceau, J. A., *Leçons de perspective positive*. Paris 1576.

Durand, J. N. L., *Precis des leçons d'architecture*. Paris 1802–1805.

Durm, J., *Die Baukunst der Griechen*. Leipzig: Kröner, 1910. First published in 1882.

Fiechter, E. R., and H. Thiersch, *Aegina, das Heiligtum der Aphaia*. Munich: Akademie der Wissenschaften, 1906.

Gibbs, J., *A Book of Architecture*. London 1728.

Guadet, J., *Elements et théorie de l'architecture I*. Paris 1901–1904.

Kohte, J., *Die Baukunst des klassichen Altertums*, Braunschweig: von Friedrich, 1915.

Krafft, J. C., and N. Ransonnette, *Plans, coupes, élévations des plus belles maisons et des hôtels construits à Paris et dans les environs*. Paris 1801–1802.

Lafever, M., *The Modern Builder's Guide*. 1883.

Ledoux, C. N., *L'architecture considérée sous le rapport de l'art des moeurs et de la législation*. Paris 1804.

Le Muet, P., *Manière de bien bâtir pour toutes sortes de personnes*. Paris 1623.

Martin, J., *Architecture ou art de bien bâtir*. Paris 1547.

Morris, R., *Lectures on Architecture*. London 1734.

Morris, R., *Rural Architecture*. London 1750.

Neufforge, J. F. de, *Recueil élémentaire d'architecture*. Paris 1757–1780.

Pain, W., *The Builder's Companion*. London 1762.

Pain, W., *British Palladio*. London 1786.

Palladio, A., *I quattro libri dell'architettura*. Venice 1570.

Patte, P., *Monuments érigés en France à la gloire de Louis XV*. Paris 1765.

Patte, P., *Mémoire sûr les objets les plus importants de l'architecture*. Paris 1769.

Percier, C., and P. F. L. Fontaine, *Palais, Maisons et autres édifices modernes dessinés à Rome*. Paris. 1798.

Perrault, C., *Les dix livres d'architecture.* Paris. 1673.

Peyre, M. J., *Oeuvres d'architecture.* Paris 1765.

Pikionis, D., "Synaisthimatiki topographia," in *To Trito Mati.* Athens 1935, 48–57.

Piranesi, F., *Antichita Romane de'Tempi della Rupubblica e de'Primi Imperatori.* 1748.

Piranesi, F., *Campo Marzio dell'Antica Roma.* 1762.

Planat, P., *Encyclopédie de l'architecture et de la construction.* Paris, undated (late nineteenth century).

Pozzo, A., *Perspectiva pictorum et architectorum Andreae Pútei e societate Jesu.* Rome 1693–1700.

Rusconi, G., *Dell'architettura.* Venice 1590.

Scamozzi, V., *Idea dell'architettura universale.* Venice 1615.

Serlio, S., *Tutte l'opere d'architettura et prospettiva di Sebastiano Serlio Bolognese.* Venice 1619. First published in 1537 (bk. I), 1540 (bk. II), 1545 (bk. III), 1547 (bk. IV), and 1575 (bk. V).

Thiersch, A., "Die Proportionen in der Architektur," in *Handbuch der Architektur.* 1889, bk. IV, ch. I.

Villalpando, J. B., "Hieronymi Pradi et Ioannis Baptistae Villalpandi e Societate Iesu," in *Ezechielem Explanationes et Apparatus Urbis ac Templi Hierosolymitani Commentariis et Imaginibus Illustratus.* Rome 1596 (I), 1604 (II), 1604 (III).

Vingboons, P., *Afbeeldsels der voornaemste gebouwen, uyt alle die Philips Vingboons geordineert heeft.* Amsterdam 1648–1674.

Ware, I., *A Complete Body of Architecture.* London 1768.

Wöfflin, H., *Renaissance und Barock.* Basel 1961. First published in 1888.

Index of Terms

Index of Names and Buildings